Costa Rica's Guide to Making Money Offshore in Bull & Bear Markets

Scott Oliver

This book is about how to invest
offshore safely, privately and profitably.
To order additional copies please
see www.amazon.com

To arrange a private consultation,
you may telephone the author
Scott Oliver
in Costa Rica at
(506) 396-3924 or see
www.offshorecostarica.com

Consultores Britanicos S.A.
Escazu, Costa Rica
Phone 011 (506) 396-3924
help@offshorecostarica.com
www.offshorecostarica.com

Copyright © 2002 by Waipalu S.A.

© All Rights Reserved. No part of this publication
may be reproduced in any form or by any means,
including photocopying, without prior
written permission of the copyright holder.

ISBN# 0-9714547-0-1

Published by Waipalu S.A.

Graphic design and layout by William Morales
Printed in Costa Rica by AI Arte e Imagen S.A.
San Jose, Costa Rica.

IMPORTANT DISCLAIMER

Disclaimer. Consultores Britanicos S.A. provides information covering many different investment funds, managed and registered in many different locations around the world. As such, laws and regulations applicable to the reader may restrict access to this information.

This information is not intended to be published or made available to any person in any jurisdiction where doing so would result in contravention of any applicable laws or regulations. Consultores Britanicos S.A. is not a law firm, nor does it provide legal advice or opinions concerning taxes, reporting or disclosure requirements, or any other requirements or obligations imposed by Costa Rica, the United States or any other jurisdiction.

The information provided by Consultores Britanicos S.A. does not constitute an offer or solicitation to sell shares or units in any of the funds referred to, by anyone in the United States of America or in which such offer, solicitation or distribution would be unlawful or in which the person making such offer or solicitation is not qualified to do so or to anyone to whom it is unlawful to make such offer or solicitation.

Applications to invest in any fund referred to must only be made on the basis of the offering document relating to the specific investment (e.g. prospectus, investment memorandum or other applicable terms and conditions). All users should consult an appropriate professional advisor as to whether they require any governmental or other consents or need to observe any formalities to enable them to invest in any particular fund and/or about the meaning of any of the information contained in written materials or within the Consultores Britanicos S.A. web site.

It is your sole responsibility to be informed of and comply with all the laws and regulations of any relevant jurisdiction that are applicable to your investment account and you agree to hold harmless Consultores Britanicos S.A. from any and all liability resulting from any such noncompliance.

Risk Statement: You should be aware of the risks associated with equity investment. Please remember that past performance is not necessarily a guide to the future. Market and currency movements may cause the value of investments and the income from them to fall as well as rise and you may get back less than you invested when you decide to sell your investments. Smaller markets can be more volatile than developed stock markets and can carry more risk. Independent financial advice should be taken before entering into any financial transaction.

Not all products or services are provided in all countries. Consultores Britanicos S.A. does not solicit or provide offerings outside its jurisdictions.

In continuing to read this book you are confirming that you have read and understood this important information.

Investing Offshore

Acknowledgments 7
Introduction 9
Preface 13

1. Shocking New Statistics Persuade More
   People To Invest Offshore 15
2. When It Sounds Too Good To Be True 19
3. Your Money Can Be Safe 'Offshore' 25
   - How Does Insurance Protect You? 27
   - Safety & Security 28
4. Costa Rica – Wall Street Journal Ranks #1 29
5. Offshore Investment Funds Are Far Less
   Taxing Than Domestic Funds 33
6. Why You Need To Own Stocks 37
7. Why You Must Own Fixed Income Funds 43
8. Did the Analysts on Wall Street Warn You? 47
9. Developing Your Investment Strategy 51
   - Examples of Point & Figure Charts 54
   - What Is Sector Rotation & How Can
     It Make Me Money? 60
   - Current Sector Analysis 63
   - What Does This Chart Tell Us?
     What Are the Six Basic Risk Levels? 65
   - What Are ETFs? How Can We Profit from
     ETFs? 69
   - Making Money When Markets Decline 72
   - Why Invest in International Markets? 74
   - Ten Steps To Investment Success 78
10. Advantages and Disadvantages of Funds 81

- Mutual Funds & Hedge Funds
  What's The Difference? 85
- How The Wealthy Stay Wealthy With Capital
  Guaranteed Hedge Funds 88
- Mistakes To Avoid in Fund Investing 90
- Which Funds Are Best For You? 94
- What Commissions & Fees Are Charged? 97
- Basic Items To Consider When
  Evaluating Any Fund 100
- What Is Dollar Cost Averaging? 102
- You Normally Get What You Pay For? 105
11. There's Always A Reason Not To Invest 107
12. Writing About Being Right & Wrong? 109
13. "Doing Business In Costa Rica" 113
    by Attorney Roger Petersen
14. "Living & Retiring in Costa Rica" 119
    by Christopher Howard
15. Frequently Asked Questions
    About Investing Offshore 123
16. Which Offshore Funds Can I Choose From? 139
    What's The Bottom Line? 142

Appendix 1 Useful Website Information 145
Appendix 2 Offshore Investor Comments 147
Appendix 3 More About The Author 152

Acknowledgements

This book has been a collaborative effort and I would like to give special thanks to my editor Tedde Thompson for all her hard work and encouragement.

My thanks to Amy Bennage in New York who has always been just wonderful. Thank you to Jon Pipas, Steve Wershing, Jonathan Davies, Jane Saunders, Georgina MacMillan, Roger Petersen, Chris Howard, Casey Halloran and, of course John Garrity, a former Wall Street colleague and the best of friends.

A special thanks to Tim Bojar of Fidelity Institutional Investments. With truly exceptional people like Tim it's no surprise that Fidelity is such a remarkably successful investment management firm.

Thanks to the tremendous work of Tom Dorsey and his team at Dorsey Wright & Associates, I came to realize that this business is without doubt, one of the most intellectually challenging and satisfying careers out there.

Last, and most important of all, I want to thank all of my wonderful clients - past, present and future - for helping to make this fascinating business so rewarding.

Scott Oliver.
Escazu, Costa Rica.

Introduction

As a Costa Rican who came back to my country of origin after spending 10 years of my professional life working with Lehman Brothers in New York City, I have learned that the biggest challenge for the development of the Costa Rican securities market is the lack of visionaries with experience and professional training, willing to come to this small country with the strong conviction of providing the Costa Rica securities market with the appropriate tools for its development.

Scott Oliver is one of these few visionaries. He has shown me that Costa Rica might become a regional financial center after all, thanks only to the efforts of professionals like him.

Scott's qualifications are those that any serious investor must require before talking to a person who calls himself a financial advisor. For many years Scott was a Registered Representative in the U.S., having passed all qualifying securities examinations (Series 7, Series 63 and Series 3). He is the President of Consultores Britanicos S.A. in Costa Rica and a foreign affiliate of a registered broker/dealer in the USA, licensed to open securities trading accounts on behalf of clients. Through this formal structure, typical in developed markets, money invested by Costa Rican investors is held by a New York Stock Exchange member firm (NYSE) and, client accounts enjoy unlimited protection including $500,000 SIPC coverage. If anything were to happen to the brokerage company or the NYSE firm that holds the client assets, you would be assured to get the value of your investments because of this coverage.

Scott has been quoted in numerous magazines and his views are highly respected by other specialists in the field. This book includes some of his views regarding investing offshore in various securities but especially offshore investment funds - an ideal investment tool for non-US citizens -- as well as an in-depth overview of relevant concepts such as investment strategies, diversification, dollar cost averaging, time spans, risk-rewards, benefits of investing in stocks over the long term and other 'must-know' concepts for every serious investor.

In short, Scott teaches us that the only way of profiting from securities is to follow a disciplined, professional investment methodology, understanding the real risks and rewards of each type of investment and accommodating such to the specific objectives and risk aversion preferences of each investor.

Scott and I share multiple projects, including establishing formal qualification requirements for financial representatives in Costa Rica and drastically increasing the sophistication of Costa Rican investors. I know his strong will and determination, together with his excellent training and qualifications, will make a big contribution towards our common goal of helping Costa Rica become a first class regional financial center. This book is an invaluable tool towards that end.

Federico Carrillo-Zurcher
Chief Executive Officer, Bolsa Nacional de Valores
(Largest Stock Exchange in Central America).

> *"For novices to come in and try to generate profit in this incredibly complex industry is like me trying to do brain surgery on the weekends to pick up a little extra cash."*
> Mark Ritchie – Professional Trader.

Preface

When I moved to Costa Rica from the Cayman Islands in 1999, it quickly became apparent that there was a lack of easily available information that clearly explained the benefits associated with investing in general, in equities - 'stocks,' in funds and, in particular, 'offshore' funds. The goal of this book is to help investors in Costa Rica to **invest offshore safely, privately and profitably**.

I have nearly 20 years of professional experience in the financial services industry in London, New York City on Wall Street, in the Cayman Islands and now Cost Rica. However, this is a business where you are learning every single day and you can never know it all. If you plan on making your own investment decisions, the information in this book should help you; however, you must have a passion for investing, for learning about the markets, for continuous studying, and the careful monitoring of all your investments.

We hope that you will learn more about disciplined offshore investing by reading this book. It is not possible to discuss everything about investing in a guide book of this size, so if you have more specific questions, please call me. This book has been a collaborative effort between seasoned professionals who specialize in offshore markets. We may not have the answers to all of your questions, but we will certainly know someone who does.

I am British so the spelling used in this document is UK English and not US English. This has been printed in English, the primary business language of the Western hemisphere.

We have a lot of information to share with you. We are confident that it will dramatically change how you view your money and the methods you use to invest. So let's get started.

Yours sincerely,

Scott Oliver

> *"You can't expect to become a doctor or an attorney overnight, and trading is no different. It is a vocation that takes time, study and experience. Wisdom is a product of knowledge and experience."*
> Mark D. Cook – Professional Trader.

1

Shocking New Statistics Persuade More People To Invest Offshore

Arranging your financial affairs to your best advantage is similar to a game of chess. But unlike chess, the rules concerning your finances are constantly changing and becoming more complicated. When you only invest in your own country (onshore), you have absolutely no financial privacy and woefully inadequate asset protection against creditors or predators. When you work with qualified offshore experts, like the Queen in a game of chess, you will enjoy the power and the freedom to move as far as you wish in any direction. Investing offshore is perfectly legal. It's the reporting requirements that can sometimes get complicated.

So investing 'offshore' simply means that you have money invested outside your own country of residence. For an investor living in Argentina, it means having money invested outside of Argentina. At present there are millions of Argentinians wishing that they had invested all of their money 'offshore.' This is not to suggest that what happened in Argentina will happen in Costa Rica however, sophisticated investors understand that 'diversification' is important with their investment portfolios and that it is also important to have some money safely invested outside their country of residence. There are other perfectly good reasons to invest offshore especially if you are doing business in the United States.

One of the 'hottest' car registration plates for attorneys in the US reads, '**All You Need is an Accident and a Dream**.' Unfortunately, this is not a joke - this is serious. According to the American Tort Reform Association, in detailing the dramatic increase in personal injury awards in the USA from 1993-1999, the median award for personal injury in New York State between 1993-1999 was $275,000. This is 96% higher than any other state and 243% higher than California ($80,000).

> *"It is estimated that 50,000 lawsuits are filed in this country (USA) every day of the week. This has come to be known as the 'litigation explosion.' Whatever the causes - a breakdown of traditional values, the loss of a sense of community, too many hungry lawyers, wasteful insurance companies - the impact on each of us is significant."* Robert J. Mintz & James J. Rubens in *Lawsuit Proof*.

In another shocking report a few years ago by the Public Policy Institute of New York State: *"The number of lawyers actively practicing in New York grew by an astounding 40% in just the last 10 years – even as the state's total population barely grew at all."*

Do you have a subsidiary of your business operating in the USA? According to the American Tort Reform Association, in detailing the dramatic increase in personal injury awards in the USA from 1993-1999, 'Business Negligence' awards rose 127% to US$1,727,220. Ever wondered why doctors charge so much? Maybe because the median 'medical malpractice' award increased by 79% to $3,495,354. 'Personal negligence' awards (which can affect practically anyone) increased by 1,089% to $2,959,047. Do you manufacture a product in the USA? 'Product liability' settlements increased by 409% to $7,360,888. It doesn't take too many of them to ruin your day.

Because of this 'litigation explosion,' many American pharmaceutical companies are thinking twice about developing new drugs (especially for children); municipalities are scared to open public parks; employers are scared of giving job references; manufacturers are refusing to develop new products; and when they do they must price all of their products higher. Some experts estimate that this 'tort tax' adds approximately $800 to the cost of having a baby and $600 extra per year to insure a car in the state of New York.

Many of these lawsuits can be described as 'frivolous lawsuits' and, according to the US Chamber of Commerce, *"Frivolous lawsuits and excessive-litigation costs US businesses and consumers US$160 billion every year."* Some of these frivolous lawsuits result in outrageous settlements and, unfortunately, **these problems are not just isolated to the US anymore, lawsuits are increasing in Costa Rica.**

Why risk it? When you can easily arrange your financial affairs so that you can achieve substantial protection from illegitimate creditors and financial predators. You can make your wealth practically invisible to others! This is why smart, careful people invest 'offshore.' By taking a few simple steps, you can avoid becoming a 'victim.'

Scott Oliver - Consultores Britanicos S.A.

2

When It Sounds Too Good To Be True....

People regularly ask for advice about various investment 'programs' that they have been introduced to, normally by a 'friend.' These 'programs' can be found in New York, London, the Cayman Islands and the Bahamas, practically everywhere! There are also a growing number of religion-based investment schemes that trick people into investing money. *"I've seen more money stolen in the name of God that in any other way,"* said Deborah Bortner of the North American Securities Administrators Association.

These 'programs' may claim to be investing in foreign currencies, in S&P futures, in real estate, in bank debentures, but the promise is invariably the same: **They all offer what appear to be extraordinarily high returns with virtually no risk**. You may be asked to sign a 'Confidentiality Agreement' so as not to divulge any proprietary information, which is quite ironic because they rarely give you information that explains exactly where or how your money is to be invested. You may be told that the investment is open to 'members only' which is their way of asking you to keep your mouth shut because what they're doing is fraudulent.

There are a few different such 'programs' available in Costa Rica. One popular 'program' is managed by a *'Tico'* (a Costa Rican) who says his business is perfectly legal in Costa Rica but has never explained to anyone exactly what his organization invests in and how it has generated returns of 3-5% per month. The 'grandfatherly businessman' says that he invests heavily in real estate and also owns a helicopter transport company. In the local English newspaper, the *'Tico Times,'* he is quoted as saying that: *"The best guarantee I can give anyone who has professional dealings with me is my clean reputation as a serious, honest and responsible businessman. Those who have had dealings with me are well aware of the guarantee that they will never, ever see me involved with anything underhanded or illicit."*

A 3-5% per monthly return is simply staggering! If he's paying that to his investors, how much are they actually making? If his 'program' is indeed legitimate, (and for the sake of their investors we sincerely hope it is), he deserves recognition because he has achieved the kind of long-term, stratospheric returns that have eluded the brightest investment and real estate managers the world has ever known. However, if someone needs their money returned does he have to run out and sell a building? How will his 'guarantee' hold up when the real estate values decline? How can we know if his 'guarantee' is good or if his 'program' is legal if he won't tell us what he is investing in? Why would anyone invest in anything when they do not know exactly how, or where their money is to be invested? Or perhaps they just don't care?

Another 'program' seen recently is a 'foreign exchange trading program.' The brochure refers to an investment of US$100K in their "10 year commitment plan" (which means you cannot take your money out) and from July

1994 - June 2000 a $100K investment would supposedly have grown to $3,055,435.70. Incidentally, this is just 60% of the profits, the other 40% is kept by the company as their share of the 'profits'. It refers to the first trading month and states that: "At the end of the first month (the company) produced a gross profit of US$26,778.10. The company allocated 40% of the profits for expenses, and the investor's shares in the 'Fund Name Withheld' 10-year plan appreciated in value by US$16,066.86. According to them this miraculous fund generated a 26% return in its first month!

In their literature, the investors' percentage of the monthly gains ranged from 0.65% all the way up to 35.27%! The world's best foreign exchange traders are right about 65% of the time yet these people are able to generate huge profits every single month without ever having a month where they lost money. And if that's only your 60% and they kept 40% of the profits as 'expenses,' this means the average return is actually closer to 8% per month.

> *"My best trader makes money only 63% of the time. Most traders make money only in the 50-55% range. That means you're going to be wrong a lot. If that's the case, you better make sure your losses are as small as they can be. And that your winners are bigger."* Steve Cohen – Professional Trader.

The people selling this program have no qualifications or experience as investment advisors. They are, in fact real, estate agents and travel agents. This program also pays you a big commission (in stock, not cash) if you bring in a 'friend' who also invests in the program. That's another warning sign!

Should you put your money into one of these 'programs?' If you cannot find out exactly what is done with your money, we would suggest that you invest your money elsewhere. **No legitimate investment advisor will refuse to explain how they will invest your money**.

Ask yourself the following basic questions:

- Who handles the money exactly?
- Where was the company formed & registered?
- Who exactly owns the company?
- Where is the company registered to do business?
- Where is the company's physical headquarters?
- Who is the President?
- Who are the other Executive Officers of the company?
- What part of the world are they from?
- What is their education and background?
- Are they qualified to do what they say they do?
- Where are the executives and the company 'registered' to do business?
- Are they and their company allowed to sell investments in Costa Rica?
- Are they licensed? If so by whom?
- How many employees do they have?
- Who and where are their traders?
- What sort of education, experience and licenses do they have?
- What exactly do they invest in?
- Whether it's currencies, S&P futures or whatever the financial instrument – what is their basic investment strategy?

- Who audits their company's track record? Otherwise how can you know they have a 'real and verifiable' track record?
- Where exactly do you send your investment money?
- With which professional bodies are the traders and the principals of the firm registered?
- Who can you call to verify this information?
- Who is the person selling you the investment 'program?' (Would you normally take investment advice from your travel agent?)
- Does the person selling the investment have any qualifications, training or experience in advising people with their investments?

Take notes of your discussions and write down the names of all of the people involved. Please don't listen to any nonsense about how the people managing the 'program' are very concerned about their 'privacy.' **Confidentiality is certainly a privilege that should be enjoyed by the client, but not by the principals of the investment firm. Find out exactly who they are**.

If you had developed a foolproof trading 'system' that could generate 8% plus per month, why would you even want other investors to invest with you? You certainly would not need them. Even if you were just a bankrupt computer genius that stumbled onto the 'system,' you wouldn't even need to find the seed capital to start trading with it. **You could sell that system for a hundred million dollars tomorrow.**

The world's biggest and best traders are widely-known and if anybody with a 'no risk, high yield' investment tells you that nobody knows their traders - that's nonsense too! When a professional places trades, makes big money and never loses money, I guarantee you that this will get noticed by the brokerage firm that's executing their trades and word will get around – fast!

There are some very smart and creative people in Costa Rica. However, how can these nameless, faceless experts generate returns that are literally three times better than the returns of the smartest, most brilliant traders anywhere else in the world? Traders who have invested hundreds of millions of dollars a year on technology, in developing incredibly complex computerized trading systems and who have years and years of experience!

Whether it's in New York, London, Hong Kong or San Jose - **any legitimate investment company will expect to be asked lots of questions, and a legitimate investment firm will also be happy to give you the answers to every single one**.

3

The Good News Is Your Money Can Be Very Safe 'Offshore'

You must do your homework when you wish to invest through an offshore firm because the rules and regulations applicable to investment advisors are invariably different.

In many countries there are few educational and training requirements necessary for someone to call themselves an 'Investment Advisor.' There are very few Central and Latin American securities markets as well regulated as most Western European countries or the USA where, by law, everyone must pass comprehensive securities examinations before they are allowed to become a 'Registered Representative.'

However, Costa Rica in particular is making serious efforts to improve its regulatory environment and the good news is that there are many professional investment advisors in Costa Rica who are well qualified. Some have even studied in the US and have passed the exact same examinations as a US 'Registered Representative.' Please do your homework and check up on whomever you are considering hiring as your investment advisor.

In visiting different international investment firms, meet the person who will be making your investment recommendations. Have them explain their investment strategy **so you understand exactly what they recommend doing with your money**. Your investments should be managed according to your individual risk and investment profile. You may feel more comfortable investing in diversified offshore investment funds instead of individual stocks.

There are thousands of offshore funds available. The 'superstar' money managers in Europe and USA often graduate up to managing their own 'offshore' fund (domiciled outside of the USA and other high tax jurisdictions) where the serious money is made. Because of this, many of the world's most successful funds are 'offshore.'

If you prefer investing only in New York Stock Exchange listed stocks, that's fine too! But find an international investment advisor who is knowledgeable about US markets and has a proven, disciplined investment strategy that will make money for you.

When it comes to safety and security, your offshore investments can benefit from the same insurance protection as they would with a major Wall Street firm. If you are an international investor presently invested in the US, you will probably feel more comfortable with an offshore investment advisor who can ensure your offshore investment account also has Securities Investor Protection Corporation (SIPC) insurance coverage to protect your assets.

Remember that you don't have to keep your money in an unknown country to become an offshore

investor. International, non-US investors living in Costa Rica can enjoy all the tax advantages of being 'offshore' even while having their assets held safely and securely by a New York Stock Exchange firm. There are a few investment firms in Costa Rica that can offer you all the advantages of being 'offshore' whilst at the same time, enjoying all the safety, security and assurances of having your assets held by a major New York Stock Exchange firm (including SIPC insurance coverage).

How Does SIPC Insurance Protect Your Assets?

Should an investor in Costa Rica wish to invest 'offshore' with an established US investment firm, the Securities Investor Protection Corporation (SIPC) is the first line of defense in the event of a US brokerage firm failure. When a US brokerage firm is closed due to fraud, bankruptcy or other financial difficulties, the Securities Investor Protection Corporation steps in as quickly as possible and, within certain limits, works to return your cash, stock and other securities you had at the firm. Without SIPC, investors at financially troubled brokerage firms might lose their securities or money forever or wait for years while their assets are tied up in court.

SIPC does not cover individuals who are sold worthless stocks and other securities. Instead, SIPC helps individuals whose money, stocks and securities are stolen by a broker or put at risk when a brokerage fails for other reasons. Customers of a failed brokerage firm get back all securities that already are registered in their name or are in the process of being registered.

To ensure that your investment account has this insurance coverage to protect your assets, the investment firm that actually holds your assets must be a "Member SIPC."

The Securities Investors Protection Act (SIPA) of 1970 is a complex and technical statute. This is only a very general description of the benefits of SIPC and we would encourage readers to get more detailed information at www.sipc.org

Safety & Security.

For maximum safety and security of your assets, you may wish to have your offshore investment account held by a major New York Stock Exchange firm where it enjoys unlimited protection, including SIPC coverage of $500,000 (This insurance coverage can include many offshore funds).

4

Costa Rica: A Growing Financial Services Centre
Wall Street Journal Ranks Costa Rica #1

O 5th October 2000, the Wall Street Journal featured a technology section about different 'less developed countries' that were trying hard to attract high-technology type companies that obviously required an intelligent, hardworking 'high-tech' workforce. Costa Rica was ranked #1 in the listing of countries to watch *"based on connectivity, information security, human capital, business climate and priority given by government to tech' business."* Why? Because there are no import taxes on computer-related equipment. Local, domestic, long-distance and wireless access rates are low. There is an aggressive government policy towards Information Technology (IT) education and improvement in intellectual property laws. With Intel's huge plant here, Costa Rica also has a strong micro-chip manufacturing industry.

Due to this focus on IT, both local and multi-national companies can benefit from improved intellectual property laws (copyrights & patents), a good level of education, and lower taxes.

Intel's gigantic operations in Costa Rica contribute a very significant amount to the gross domestic product of the country. No doubt Intel considered the points previously mentioned critical in their decision to start operations in Costa Rica. Many other multi-national companies such as Microsoft, Procter & Gamble, Lucent and Bristol Myers have taken advantage of the Costa Rican IT level and many additional companies are considering further investments within this beautiful and politically stable Central American country.

The telephone rates in Costa Rica are among the cheapest in Central America and more and more Costa Rican businesses are now using the Internet as an effective communications, sales and marketing tool.

The offshore investment community in Costa Rica is growing rapidly. It is happening because there is considerably less bureaucratic burden and unnecessary legal expense. In other words, it is efficient. Business will always flow to the most efficient environment and money will always go where it's treated best.

> Warren Buffett said; *"I used to feel when I worked back in New York that there were more stimuli just hitting me all the time, and if you've got the normal amount of adrenaline, you start responding to them. It may lead to crazy behavior after a while. It's much easier to think here."* Needless to say, Omaha, Nebraska (where he is based), is a long way from Costa Rica but when it comes to advising you on the management of your money, the same principle applies. Costa Rica

> has everything that a sophisticated, international investor needs in a global financial center. It's a beautiful, stable and peaceful country with good privacy laws, hard working, qualified professionals who will ensure that your assets are protected properly, and zero taxes for those international investors who make their profits outside of Costa Rica.

Costa Rica has everything that a sophisticated, international investor needs in a global financial center. It's a beautiful, stable and peaceful country with good privacy laws, hard working, qualified professionals who will ensure that your assets are protected properly, and zero taxes for those international investors who make their profits outside of Costa Rica.

Companies like **Intel, Procter & Gamble, Abbott Labs, Bristol Myers, Chiquita Brands, Texaco, 3M, UPS, DHL, Gillette, Warner Lambert, Xerox, Glaxo Smithkline, Johnson & Johnson, SC Johnson, Sherwin Williams, Sony Music, Pfizer, Kimberly Clark, Manpower, Microsoft, Dole Fresh Fruit, Colgate Palmolive, LL Bean, Alcatel, BASF, Lucent, KPMG, Price Waterhouse, Deloitte & Touche, 3 Com, Motorola, Oracle, Western Union, Unisys and Cisco Systems** have made huge investments in Costa Rica. It is estimated that non-Costa Rican companies invested over US$600 million in Costa Rica just in the year 2000.

5

'Offshore' Investment Funds Are Far Less Taxing Than Domestic Funds

Looking in the *Financial Times* or the *International Herald Tribune*, you can see that there are thousands of offshore funds, many of which will sound familiar: Fidelity, LM Global, Putnam, Janus, Morgan Stanley Dean Witter and many more. Fidelity alone has US$1.6 billion invested in their many offshore funds. Putnam and LM Global both have over US$1 billion invested in their various offshore funds. This is big business!

New offshore investors become very excited when they discover the significant and many 'rich' advantages of investing in well-managed offshore funds compared to investing in the domestic funds offered by a US - based investment advisor.

International investors may be content investing in regular, domestic funds. They may be content with paying taxes that they don't need to pay, but more often than not, they simply don't know what's really available? The world's best offshore funds are not available to investors US or Canadian residents. (These funds are certainly available to Canadian investors legally resident in Costa Rica). **Therefore, if you are a Costa Rican investor investing with a 'traditional' US or Canadian**

investment firm, you do not have access to many of the world's best money managers.

Working with qualified offshore professionals, you can enjoy a level of financial privacy simply unheard of onshore, far superior asset protection, access to some of the world's best money managers and -- depending on your nationality -- zero taxes.

Some fund managers manage domestic and offshore funds, but because of the significant tax advantages of being 'offshore' you will normally end up with a lot more money in your pocket than you would do if you invested in their domestic fund equivalent.

Unlike onshore funds that must report the names of all their investors, offshore funds do not report ownership so there are also 'asset protection' benefits associated with owning 'offshore' funds as well as significant tax benefits.

If you're an international investor working with an offshore investment advisor who has the right connections, you can easily electronically transfer an existing 'domestic US' brokerage account to a special 'offshore' investment account so that you can invest in these offshore funds.

> *"If you are a long term investor, your greatest enemies are inflation and taxes, not short term market fluctuations."* "New Rules For Financial Success" by Jonathan Clements.

Your average US fund manager trades stocks actively in an effort to maximize pre-tax returns. This is normally done without thinking about what taxes

the individual investor must pay. This applies to Costa Rican and other non-US and international investors when they invest. After signing the W8Ben form, the Costa Rican investor will NOT pay taxes on long-term capital gains tax distributions made by the fund (maximum federal rate of 20%). However, **the investor in Costa Rica will pay taxes on short-term capital gains distributions and, if they own individual stocks, they will also lose 30% in withholdings on all US securities dividends and interest income. What could be worse? If the Costa Rican or international investor dies tomorrow, his estate would be taxed at graduated rates from 26% to as much as 55%.** (There's an exemption only on the first $60K of US assets).

These taxes apply to the year-end distributions (reinvested or taken in cash) that are made by US funds. Funds generate capital gains and income for shareholders by selling investments that have increased in price and by earning dividends and interest on its investments. If you are a non-US investor investing in US funds, you will pay taxes on short-term capital gains distributions of up to 39.6% that would be paid on all stocks sold at a profit by the fund within a year of purchase.

According to the *Wall Street Journal* of August 6th 2001: *"Last year, capital gains distributions by funds hit a record $345 billion, even though the average stock fund had a loss of 4.5%"* The SEC says that ***"taxes cut more than 2.5% from the average stock fund's annual total return."*** So what if you only manage to keep an extra 1%? As of 31st December 2000 the S&P 500 was up 17.46% per annum over the previous ten years. If Javier invested $250K ten years ago and enjoyed 17.46% per annum and Jose only earned 16.46% during the same period. That 1% difference means an extra US$102,416.87 in your pocket after only 10 years. **What could you do with an extra $102,416.87?** There are many North Americans that have retired on less than that here in Costa Rica!

So now you know why sophisticated, well-informed Costa Rican investors are investing in secure, 'offshore' funds and not domestic US funds. Because they avoid all of these taxes and they avoid losing up to 55% of their assets to Uncle Sam in estate taxes. Since profits will be made outside of Costa Rica, there will be no taxes applicable inside Costa Rica. **For Costa Rican and most non-US investors this means 100% legal tax-free investing whilst having some of the best fund managers in the world managing your money!**

Many of the biggest US funds from Fidelity, Putnam, Janus, Morgan Stanley Dean Witter and LM Global offer offshore funds that are managed by the same people that manage the US fund. Fidelity alone has over US$1 billion invested in their offshore funds. It's like looking at two new cars, both exactly the same except one has far superior fuel consumption than the other. This means that **one of those cars will get you to your destination with a lot more gas left in your tank than the other. The question is: Are you driving the right car?**

The United States is the biggest tax haven of all but, and this is a big 'but,' not if you are a US citizen. **Not everyone can invest offshore tax-free**, but the tax deferred compounding of ordinary income, interest income, dividends and capital gains is a very powerful advantage when accumulating assets internationally. **It's an easy decision! When you invest in offshore funds, your assets are protected; your financial life is private; and you enjoy significant tax advantages with access to the world's best money managers.**

6

Why You Need To Own Stocks or Stock Investment Funds for Growth

Believe it or not, it's fairly simple to accumulate wealth over the long-term through a disciplined investment strategy in funds that invest primarily in common stocks. The newspapers and magazines want you to believe that it's difficult, but it's not. The reality is that if you consistently invest a fixed dollar amount every single month (in strong and weak markets) in well-managed, diversified funds, **over the long-term** you will accumulate wealth. Wealth is not always determined by investment performance, it is often determined by investor behaviour. **Sometimes the key to making money owning good stocks is not getting scared out of them.**

People greatly overestimate the risk in owning stocks over the long-term and they underestimate the risk of not owning stocks. History shows that the long-term advance in the stock market is permanent. It's the declines that are temporary and you really don't want stocks to go much higher until you've finished buying, right?

Put time on your side! According to an Ibbotson research report published in December 2001, if you take a look at the S&P 500 index from 1926-2001 you will see the percentage of time where stocks showed positive returns over different time periods. Over a one year period, the S&P 500 moved higher 71% of the time, over five year periods the S&P 500 has moved higher 90% of the time, 10 years? 97% of the time with 15 & 20 year periods the S&P 500 has moved higher 100% of the time.

Do we really need to fear this 'risk' in owning stocks? Managing risk is a challenge; however, effective risk management is where the opportunity lies because 'risk' means different things to different people. I recently asked a group of tourists how they felt about the drive across the mountains in a bus to Jaco Beach on the west coast of Costa Rica. Most of them were fine; some had been scared; one had taken tranquilizers; and two of them had slept all the way. People rarely feel the same way about risk throughout their lives.

This is good! If everyone valued risk in the same way, there would be no opportunities. Some people place great importance on the small probability of big profits and others are more concerned with preservation of capital and do not want to take any risks. When one sees the glass 'half-empty, another may see it 'half-full' and they are both correct!

Many people new to investing just cannot imagine owning stocks that can move substantially higher. 2002 has been a very challenging year in the US stockmarkets but there are always opportunities. As an example we have included the top 40 'movers' in the New York Stock Exchange in the first three months of 2002 up to 29th March 2002. Yes folks! Some people actually owned these stocks:

NYSE Listed Company	Last Price	3 Month % Growth
Hecla Mining pfB	20.00	147.8
Boyd Gaming	15.04	131.4
JoAnnStrs A	16.14	125.7
Sports Auth	11.50	101.8
JoAnnStrs B	12.95	94.70
Shopko Str	18.10	90.50
TRW pfD	375.00	78.60
Ducommun	19.70	77.50
Alltrista	27.55	75.50
Hanger Ortho	10.35	72.50
WhthlJwlr	18.85	71.50
Wackenhut B	32.57	71.10
Chiquita Brd pfB	8.60	70.30
Owens Illinois	17.00	70.20
Dave Busters	10.40	65.60
Aaron Rent A	22.05	63.30
Iron Mtn	31.72	62.90
Dept 56	14.00	62.80
Sierra Hlth	13.08	61.50
Action Perf	49.25	60.90
Marinemax	12.00	59.20
Tower Auto	13.99	54.90
Dana Cp	21.47	54.70
Labor Rdy	7.80	52.60
Std Regstr	28.12	51.80
Templtn Rus	27.10	50.50
Dillards	23.86	49.10
Rock Tenn A	21.45	49.00
Station Cno	16.65	48.80
Ipsco	17.09	48.60
Pennz Quak	21.47	48.60
Penn Am Gp	15.64	48.20
Benchmk Elec	28.00	47.70
MSC Sftwr	23.00	47.40
Ros Tele	7.73	47.20

The most powerful tools of risk management ever to be invented are the laws of probability. A simple example would be insurance companies using probabilities to calculate the odds of people dying at various ages so that they can stay in business and make money with their insurance products. The key to effective risk management is maximizing the areas where we have some control over the outcome while minimizing the areas where we have absolutely no control over the outcome.

We must remember, however, that real wealth goes to the 'owners' of great companies, not the 'lenders' to great companies. Equities or stocks are nothing more than a share in the ownership of a business. Many Costa Rican investors feel 'safer' loaning their money to a bank. If you examine the facts, we think you will agree that 'owning' rather than 'loaning' is far more lucrative! Risk is not allowing your portfolio to grow to it's full potential. **The greatest risk any of us will ever face is outliving our money**, which is what we'll look at next.

Why You Should Not Be Scared of the Market

So let's get it out of the way right now and talk about the stock market 'crash.' Like the price of coffee, stock markets go up and down, sometimes slow and often fast; it's all part of the 'market.' Let's see what happened to two wealthy Costa Ricans who both invested US$1 million dollars **one month before** the 1987 stock market 'crash.'

Mario is an old-fashioned investor who wants 'safe' investments and one day after the 'crash' he is very pleased with himself because he invested in 'safe and insured' bank certificates of deposit in the US.

Pier is a younger, more 'progressive' investor. He had invested the exact same amount on the same day as Mario, but Pier had invested 60% of his money in the diversified smaller equities in the Russell 2000 index and 40% in the equities of some of the world's biggest companies listed in the S&P 500. When Pier saw the markets tumbling, all he could do was pray! His grandfather had warned him that stocks were 'risky' and now look what happened!

However, let's fast forward to the 31st December 2001, which is fourteen years later, and see how their portfolios compare. Unfortunately, not only did Pier suffer in the 'crash,' he didn't monitor his portfolio either and his stocks also declined dramatically in 2000 & 2001.

Fourteen years later, Mario's 'safe' investments have earned him an average annual total return of 5.61% and he has US$2,187,482 in the bank. (He reinvested all dividends and received no income).

During the exact same period, Pier had enjoyed 9.21% per annum on his stocks in the Russell 2000 which produced US$2,123,056. Pier also enjoyed 11.82% per annum in his S&P 500 stocks which adds another US$1,985,214 for a grand total of US$4,108,270 **That's nearly $2 million more than Mario!**

It would appear that old-fashioned investors simply cannot handle the idea of investing their money in equities. That is fine! Equities are not for everyone! If you are going to need the money within five years then you probably should not invest in stocks or stock mutual funds. Younger, more 'progressive' and 'global' individuals have seen many of their foreign friends from college make 'serious money' in the stock market. Unfortunately, it's all so easy to make excuses not to invest, to delay until you finish your studies or get that promotion, or after the wedding, after your son is born... In this example, Pier invested in stocks one month before the October 1987 crash. During this period, there was the Gulf War, the Asian economic crisis, some of the worst years in the US stock market history. We had so many 'disasters' that at the time the newspapers would have you believe that it was the end of the world!

Any major market decline is painful for investors who own stocks, but **the long-term bottom line results speak for themselves - Pier has accumulated nearly US$2 million more than Mario!** Don't you think you should explore what may be possible for you and your family when you invest in equities over the long-term? Your cost of living will probably triple after you retire. Do you know of any other strategy that has the potential to triple your income during retirement?

This is why most sophisticated investors believe that the real long-term risk of equities is NOT owning them.

7

Why You Must Also Own Fixed Income Funds

Fixed income funds are also an important part of your portfolio. More often than not, when the stock market has a tough time (as it has in the last two years) you will notice that well managed, top quality fixed income funds will perform well because investors are looking for a 'safe' place away from the stock market's volatility and they tend to invest in more secure government bonds. The opposite applies, when the stock market is looking attractive after a decline, fixed income funds tend to see money move out of the more secure fixed income type investments into more aggressive, high growth opportunities in the stock market.

Fixed income funds are made up of individual bonds. Bonds are debt securities similar to an I.O.U. When you invest in bonds, you are actually lending your money to a government, a corporation or another entity that promises to pay you a specific rate of interest during the life of the bond and then to repay you the face value of the bond at maturity.

Depending on your overall investment objectives, you might have only 10% of your money invested in fixed income. you may have 100% of your money invested in fixed income. For older investors who may need access to their money within five years or, for investors that simply cannot handle the emotional turmoil of owning stocks, fixed income funds may be the best place to invest.

There are many factors that have to be taken into consideration when investing in bonds of any kind. Interest rates are obviously important but the maturity, the redemption features of individual bonds and the credit quality are crucially important and the mathematics of calculating the 'current yield', the 'yield to maturity' and 'yield to call' can be overwhelming which is why many investors prefer to allow a fixed income expert to choose the bonds held within a fund.

There are numerous fixed income funds that you may wish to consider. Some funds may invest in government securities, corporate bonds, mortgages, asset backed securities, federal agency securities and even foreign government bonds. Speaking of foreign government bonds Mr. 'Costa Rican Investor', please allow me to ask you a question: Would you consider investing in the government bonds of Botswana, Tunisia, Trinidad or Korea? Perhaps you would prefer to think of investing in the government bonds of Greece, Thailand, Poland or Malaysia? Do you feel that Costa Rican US dollar government bonds are a 'safe' investment?

As you may know, amongst other things Standard and Poors (S&P) issues 'credit ratings' which is their opinion of the creditworthiness of an obligor with respect to a specific financial obligation. It takes into consideration the creditworthiness of guarantors, insurers, or other forms of credit enhancement on the obligation and takes into account the currency in which the obligation is denominated. These credit ratings are based on current information furnished by the obligors or obtained by S&P from other sources it considers reliable.

Conservative investors who do not like to take any risks with their money would only invest in bonds with an 'investment grade' rating. S&P has the 'AAA' rating as the highest rating where the issuer shows an excellent capacity to service and repay debt. 'AA' is the same capacity but to a lesser degree. 'A' is considered a strong capacity to service and repay debt normally, but vulnerable to the external environment and to technical changes.

Most investors in Costa Rica consider themselves 'extremely conservative,' they believe that when their money is invested in the US dollar government bonds of Costa Rica that they are 'safe' and they not taking any risk. However, **the bonds of Costa Rica are not considered 'investment grade' or 'safe' by anyone outside of Costa Rica, in fact, they are considered 'somewhat speculative' and carry significantly more risk than the government bonds of Botswana (A+), Tunisia (A) or Korea (A+) which are rated 'investment grade.'** The Costa Rica soccer team may have beaten Trinidad however, even the government bonds of Trinidad (BBB+) are considered 'investment grade' and are less risky than Costa Rica's government bonds.

S&P gives a 'speculative grade' rating of 'BB+' to Costa Rica which means an 'increasing uncertainty surrounding service and repayment of debt. Debt carries an increasing degree of risk.' Costa Rican government bonds carry an 'increasing degree of risk,' are speculative and not 'safe.' Based on this information, conservative, risk averse investors may wish to re-examine their portfolios to ensure that their 'conservative' money is not invested in what they think are 'safe' investments when in fact they are 'speculative.' Should you wish more detailed information on credit ratings, please see www.standardandpoors.com

As always, the management of the fund and the historical track record must be carefully examined. One fund that is particularly popular amongst sophisticated Costa Rican investors is managed by Bill Gross. You can see Bill Gross speaking on CNBC television practically every week because he is considered by many experts to be the best fixed income manager in the USA. He also manages an offshore fund that has the exact same investment objectives as his USA fund (which has over $50 billion invested) and has averaged about 8% per annum over the past ten years. As always, you obviously need to do your homework to see if this fund is suitable for you.

8

Did the Analysts on Wall Street Warn You?

Included below is a summary of the year 2000 'Recommended Lists' of a few of the biggest Wall Street investment firms. A 'Recommended List' is the list of stocks that an investment firm believes has the best prospects for making their clients money.

According to the Wall Street Journal, First Union Securities 'Recommended List' had the worst track record - down 38.3% for the year 2000 and up only 27.4% over the past five years.

Investment Firm	**Year 2000**
First Union Securities	Down 38.3%
Prudential Securities	Down 22.5%
Lehman Brothers	Down 22%
Salomon Smith Barney	Down 15.7%
Bear Stearns	Down 14.3%
Morgan Stanley	Up 1%
Goldman Sachs	Up 9.6%
Merrill Lynch	Up 12.3%
S&P 500 Index	Down 7.8%

The years 2000/2001 were not very profitable years for the average stock investor and especially the owners of technology and Internet-related stocks.

According to a recent Securities & Exchange Commission study (July 2001), it was discovered that around 28% of brokerage analysts *"owned stock in companies they cover before the businesses went public, and some made as much as $3.5 million by selling shares while they were telling investors to buy."* The SEC Acting Chairman stated *"It has become clear that research analysts are subject to several influences that may affect the integrity and the quality of their analysis and recommendations."*

> *"If a brokerage firm earns several million dollars doing an underwriting for a stock, it is very difficult for an analyst of that firm to issue anything other than a buy rating, even if he believes the company has significant problems."* Steve Watson – Professional Trader.

Did the analysts on Wall Street warn you? Rarely! Remember that the Wall Street investment firms are in the business of distribution. They need to move stock down through the system. They typically make huge fees on mergers, acquisitions and Initial Public Offerings (IPOs) and huge money personally in the IPO if they own the stock, but only if the 'product' is eventually sold to you, the investor.

What does this mean? It means the brokerage firms must sell its own 'products' and 'recommendations' to you to stay profitable in a very competitive business and that doesn't necessarily mean that it is a good investment for you. This is one of the most important reasons why you need to understand what you are doing when you invest or find an independent, objective, qualified, professional investment advisor that you can trust.

In April of 2000 when the market really started to crack, First Call/Thomson Financial said that out the 28,000 stock recommendations they track, approximately 67% were 'Buys,' 32% were 'Neutral,' and 0.9% were 'Sells.' When so many stocks were being slaughtered, Wall Street analysts were recommending that you 'Buy' 67% of the stocks they followed and 'Sell' only 0.9% of them. Following that advice would not have helped you make money. It won't do your investment account any good to blame the analysts, but **having a solid risk management plan has always been -- and will always be -- one of the most important things you must adhere to when investing.**

On Wall Street, some professional analysts have earned their reputations by being able to find the needle in a haystack and 'pick' winning stocks. Henry Blodget from Merrill Lynch created quite a stir when he correctly predicted that the stock of the Internet bookseller Amazon.com would go to $400 per share. After this feat he was considered quite an influential analyst.

> *"The irony is that, with few exceptions, the same factors that make an industry exciting also make it a potentially ruinous investment because it will attract excess financial and intellectual capital."* Michael Lauer – Professional Trader.

In early August 2000, Henry Blodget downgraded 11 of the 29 Internet stocks he followed closely. The downgrades came after these stocks had already been devastated. As examples, Pets.com and Buy.com had each fallen about 90% from their one year highs. Blodget also downgraded eToys, which had fallen 95% from its highs. However, many investors feel that this downgrading was a little too late. The downgrade would have been more useful for investors before these stocks imploded.

Picking winning stocks is very difficult indeed, as most investors have discovered. It is important to know when to buy a stock or fund, but **it is also important to know when to sell a stock or fund**. Even if you are a long-term buy - and - hold type investor, holding onto any investment and watching it tumble 90-95% lower is simply insane.

Successful investing requires a proven investment strategy that you stick to religiously, you must have strict rules that you follow regarding taking profits and you must ensure that you manage your risk carefully.

Many investors should not buy individual stocks at all; they simply cannot handle it emotionally. They buy high and sell low, holding onto the losers and selling the winners when they should be doing the opposite. These investors should definitely consider investing in some of the many offshore investment funds that are available. That way, you can focus on doing the things you love and enjoy whilst having some of the world's best professional money managers managing your money

9

Developing Your Investment Strategy

There are numerous trading methods and systems. However, there is no 'holy grail.' There is no 'secret' system that will make you ridiculously wealthy. **It boils down to a lot of very hard work, developing a disciplined investment strategy combined with a solid risk management system whilst trading or investing in something that suits your emotional profile**. Emotions make a up a very big part of the money game and if it does not 'feel right' to you then you'll never make serious money.

As an example we would like to examine an investment strategy we use which is actually quite simple. Note that I said 'simple' and not 'easy.'

It is easy to find information on which publicly traded companies are fundamentally sound. In fact, there's too much information out there. It is far more difficult to find information on when exactly you should buy and then eventually sell a stock or a fund.

One of the oldest charting systems is called 'Point & Figure' charting. This is where the intra-day price changes provide supply and demand information that is absolutely essential to the formation of trend data, which in turn leads to "Buy" and "Sell" decisions. Price changes simply reflect the tug-of-war between buyers and sellers – the strength of one or the other will be the ultimate determination of the stock's price. If you have more buyers than sellers (demand), the price rises. If you have more sellers than buyers (supply), the price declines. On the actual chart you will see that demand is reflected with an 'X' whereas supply is reflected with a 'O.'

This may seem obvious, but few methods show this as clearly as point and figure charting. All other factors remain irrelevant. Charts will accurately register the balance of power between these opposing forces.

In a study done by Professor Earl Davis of Purdue University concerning the profitability associated with different chart patterns, you will notice the following probabilities: (The table overleaf is reproduced from AW Cohen's book <u>Three Point Reversal Method of Point & Figure Technical Analysis</u>.)

Bull Market Results			
Chart Pattern	**% Probability**	**Average Gain**	**Months Duration**
Double Top	80.30	38.70	11.50
Triple Top	87.90	28.70	6.80
Spread Triple Top	85.70	22.90	7.70
Bullish Triangle	71.40	30.90	5.40
Bullish Signal	80.40	26.50	8.60
Bearish Signal Reversal	92.00	23.20	2.50
Combinations	79.50	36.90	8.00
Bear Market Results			
Double Bottom	82.10	22.70	4.70
Triple Bottom	93.50	23.00	3.40
Spread Triple Bottom	86.50	24.90	4.60
Bearish Triangle	87.50	33.30	2.50
Bearish Signal	88.60	21.90	4.90
Combinations	83.30	22.90	3.40

(There are many different types of chart patterns)

In looking at these charts, you will quickly realize that for nimble traders there are as many opportunities to make money when the market goes down as there are when the market goes higher. If you compare the results from both bull and bear markets which you can see in the chart below, you will see that there is actually less risk in selling short in a bear market than buying in a bull market. So traders that do not sell short in a bear market are ignoring low risk, high probability trades. Traders must learn to adjust their thinking to make money both in bull and in bear markets.

	Bull Market	Bear Market
Profitable	83.7%	86.9%
Average Gain	29.5%	24.8
Average Time	7.2 months	3.9 months

You may ask: 'How on earth do I keep track of all these charts?' The answer is: You don't need to if you don't want to. Most investors do not have the time to create their own charts. However, **you can subscribe to different levels of point & figure charting services by clicking on http://www.dorseywright.com where you can find practically any point and figure chart you want**. You can even sign on for a free 14-day trial. Try creating your own charts with the help of the comprehensive 'PnF University,' where you can learn how to develop your own 'high-probability' investment strategy.

Special Limited Offer: My friends at Dorsey Wright & Associates have promised me that when you mention this book when you subscribe to the 'Charts Plus' and 'Mutual Fund' service for $45 per month, after the first three months, you will receive the fourth month free! This special offer is only available until 12/31/02.

'Point & Figure' Chart Examples

Triple Top

60							
59						X	
58						X	
57		X		X		X	
56		X	O	X	O	X	
55		X	O	X	O	X	
54		X	O	X	O		
53		X	O				
52		X					
51		X					
50		X					
49							

The rising 'tops' show that buying is increasing until it breaks through a 'Triple Top,' which is a high probability 'Buy' signal. This chart could be of a stock, a mutual fund, an Exchange Traded Fund, a specific index or any other financial instrument. The rising 'bottoms' tell us that the selling is slowing.

Triple Bottom

38							
37		X					
36		X	O				
35		X	O	X			
34		X	O	X	O	X	
33		X	O	X	O	X	O
32		X	O	X	O	X	O
31		X	O		O		O
30							O
29							O
28							

The lower 'tops' show that buying is decreasing.

The lower 'bottoms' show us there is more selling; the stock weakens until it breaks through a 'Triple Bottom' at $30 which is a very high probability 'Sell' signal. If you owned this stock, to protect profits or prevent losses, you might consider placing an automatic sell order here at around $30.25.

Triangle

A bullish or bearish 'Triangle' formation can form. With an upward trending pattern the 'breakout' would tend to be higher as in this example at $53 and above. In a downward trending pattern the 'breakout' tends to be lower as at $50 and below.

57								
56	X							
55	X	O						
54	X	O	X					
53	X	O	X	O				
52	X	O	X	O	X			
51	X	O	X	O	X			
50	X	O	X	O				
49	X	O	X					
48	X	O						
47	X							
46	X							
45								

Dow Jones US Healthcare Index - IYH

69																								X	O	X
68																							X		A	O	X
67																							X	O	X	O	X
66																							7	O	X	O	
65																							X	O	X		
64																							X	O	X		
63																							X	O	X		
62																							X	8	X		
61																							6	9			
60																							X				
59		4																					5				
58		X	O														X						X				
57		X	O														2	O					4				
56		3	O	X					X				X			X	X	O					X				
55		2	O	X	O			7		X	O			B	O	X	O					X				
54		X	O	X	O	6		X	O	X	O	X		X	O	X	O	X				X				
53	O	X	O	X	5	X	O	X	O	X	9	A	O	X	C	X	3	X	O	X						
52	O	X	O		O	X	O	X	O	X	O	X	O	X	O	X	O	X	O	X						
51	1			O		O		8	X	O	X	O		O	X	O		O								
50								O		O		1														
49																											

With the IYH index you can clearly see that from January 2000 (months are indicated with numbers - January is #1 month on the chart) through January 2001 the chart has a fairly narrow trading range between $50-$57. Then in early May 2001 it 'breaks out' at $58 and doesn't really look back until late December (not shown) when it reaches $73. If you can consistently catch 25% moves like this from $58-$73, you will be a very successful investor.

As always, having the patience to wait for these trades to develop is crucial. It's important to note that investing is often as much art as it is science. Even if you really are a 'brilliant' world-class trader, you may be making money with your trades about 65% of the time, which obviously means that you will not make money about 35% of the time. So you must manage your risk carefully. Nothing is guaranteed! Based on these studies, however, the odds are in your favor if you wait for a high probability chart pattern to form before making an investment. With the help of this point and figure charting system and other important indicators, investors usually enjoy consistent 'high probability' results.

> *"The essential element is that the markets are ultimately based on human psychology, and by charting the markets you're merely converting human psychology into graphic representations."* Al Weiss – Professional Trader.

This is not the only investment strategy that works. There are, obviously, thousands of different investment strategies; however, you must find one that is both emotionally and financially suitable to you.

What Condition Is The Market In?

Understanding when to time the purchase and sale of your investments underlying the various industry sectors can help your bottom line tremendously. Most investors try to make things more complicated than they need to be and overlook simple market indicators that have worked for years. The '**New York Stock Exchange Bullish Percent**' (NYSEBP) is one such indicator and answers the question "What Condition Is The Market In?' The NYSEBP indicator was created by Chartcraft in 1955.

If it will help, think of a soccer game when you look at the market. **Like a soccer game, there is a time to be offensive (when you buy stocks) and a time to be defensive on the field (when you sell, sell short or protect profits in the stocks you own).** The NYSE Bullish Percent Index can be instrumental in helping investors measure the prevailing risk in the market place. Understanding which team to have on the field (offensive or defensive) is the key to risk management. In other words, **risk perception is the key to risk management**. We follow the large industry sectors very closely. We **use this index to determine how 'overbought' (too high) or 'oversold' (too low) the market is.**

The NYSE Bullish Percent has been one of the best at calling intermediate market tops and bottoms since its inception in 1955. It is based on the percent of stocks on the NYSE that have bullish point and figure charts. If there are 2,000 stocks on the NYSE and 600 of those stocks have buy signals on their point and figure charts and 1,900 have sell signals, then the NYSE Bullish Percent is at 30%. In the case of an industry sector, if there are 100 stocks in the sector and 30 are on buy signals the Sector Bullish Percent would be at 30%.

A stock is considered 'bullish' if its last signal was a 'buy' (the last columns of X's – 'demand' - exceeds a previous column of X's). A stock is considered 'bearish' if the last signal was a sell (the last column of O's – 'supply' - exceeds a previous column of O's). When the majority of stocks are giving 'buy' signals, it is a sign that the sector is supporting higher prices and, if the majority of stocks are giving 'sell' signals it is a sign that the sector is no longer supporting stock prices. This is especially true when you might see conflicting signals for example, the Dow Jones could be making new highs and the Sector Bullish Percent is in a clear decline.

The best 'sell' signals are given when the Bullish Percent rises above the 70% level and reverses down 6% to below the 70% level. The other clear sell signal on the chart overleaf is the box shaded (at the #6 in the early 1998) where the NYSEBP falls through a spread triple bottom. The Bullish Percent is a leading indicator so the Dow will typically continue rising after many of the Sector Bullish Percent's have reversed.

The best 'buy' signals are given when the index declines below the 30% level and reverses up 6% to above the 30% level (As indicated by the four shaded boxes in the chart overleaf). In many cases the truth lies somewhere in between. When 'sell' signals are given, it suggests that not enough stocks are participating to keep the upward move in motion. When 'buy' signals are given more stocks are changing from negative to positive chart configurations. This suggests that some sort of sector 'bottom' has been reached and the probability is higher prices for the sector.

On the page below you will find the New York Stock Exchange Bullish Percent Indicator as of the end of 2001 showing a turnaround in process.

What Is Sector Rotation? How Can It Make Me Money?

The economy can be divided into hundreds of industries. Many of these industries are quite similar and can be combined to form a sector. For example, the technology sector presently consists of more than a dozen industries. **In using 'sector rotation,' an investor attempts to avoid the worst performing sectors and tries to invest in the sectors he feels will perform better**. Everything moves in cycles. Economies, industries, stock markets and their different sectors. If you are good at picking good stocks, you'll be even more profitable if you stick to the best sectors and, of course, you can sometimes do this with less risk and volatility by investing in specific sector funds. For example, you may wish to focus on telecommunications, biotechnology, healthcare, real estate, a specific country or index.

Let's look at four different hypothetical investors in a study done by CDA Weinberger. Each used a different strategy and invested $1,000 between 1983-1998.

Mr. 'Buy & Hold' started with $1,000 and simply bought the S&P 500 that appreciated to $11,817. Mr. 'Market Timer' was practically clairvoyant and was invested in the S&P 500 for every month that it rose and was not invested in any month when the S&P 500 declined. The account of Mr. 'Market Timer' rose to $73,373. The third investor, Mr. 'Sector Picker,' was also clairvoyant enough to know which sectors would be the best performing sector in each year. He was invested in the best performing sector every year and his account grew to $115,006 during the same period. The fourth and last investor invested in the worst performing sector every year and he ended up with only $172.

The economic activity and stock prices of these industry sectors can move independently of other sectors and often independent of the market itself. It would appear that 60% of a stock's price movement is determined by the general trend of the market. Thirty per cent of a stock's movement is determined by the trend of the industry or the stock's sector and only 10% of a stock's movement is due to reasons specific to the company itself.

This means that about 90% of a stock's price performance is determined by the strength or weakness of the market and its specific sector. **The key to making money** is to look at sectors the same way that you would look at a specific stock. Try to find a sector that has clearly 'bottomed,' wait patiently to make sure that it has started to move higher and develops into a 'high-probability' chart pattern, and then invest in a sector fund or the specific leading stocks within that sector as it recovers. **You must find the courage to buy stocks in sectors that are out of favour which can be difficult since it goes against human nature**.

For many investors however, sector rotation is too much work and they prefer to be fully invested at all times. As long as they don't get 'scared' out of the market they can still do well. In a recent study of the S&P 500 by Ned Davis Research looking at the ten-year period from the end of December 1991 to the end of December 2001 it **concluded that if you remained fully invested in the S&P 500 at all times during this period your annualized return for all trading days would have been 12.9%**. If you were out of the market for the best 10 days, your return drops to 8.1% per annum. If you missed the best 20 days, it falls to 4.7% per annum. If you were out of the market for the best 30 days, it drops to 1.9% per annum and if you missed the best 40 days, your annualized return drops to a negative –0.5%.

It's not always easy to identify sectors that have reached a 'bottom' or a 'low.' We use the same charting methodology that shows us where the supply and demand is with an individual stock. This system helps us to identify sectors that appear ready to move up or down.

If you are willing to dedicate some serious time to your research, sector investing can make it fairly simple for investors to focus on specific industries they feel are poised for growth and where their success will not depend on just one stock. You can make money with this strategy either by identifying the leading individual stocks in a strong sector or, should you prefer, you could invest in an ETF (Exchange Traded Fund) or a mutual fund specializing in that sector. Just as importantly, you can protect your hard earned profits by identifying sectors that are weakening and selling off those stocks or funds before they fall further.

Risk management is extremely important, especially when many markets seem to move from one extreme to another. Markets move in cycles. Sectors and individual stocks rise and fall and, as you will see everyday on the television, there are numerous catalysts that can force a stock lower. Investors should not become complacent and assume that their stocks will keep on moving higher. The wise investor knows better and tries to expect the unexpected.

> *"If you don't stay with your winners, you are not going to be able to pay for the losers."*
> Michael Marcus – Professional Trader.

We have included a recent example of the 'Sector Analysis' that we follow.

Sector Analysis March 2002

Sector	Status	Date	Level
NYSE Bull Percent	Bull Confirmed	3/12/02	66%
Optionable Stocks	Bear Alert	3/04/02	62%
OTC Bull Percent	Bull Confirmed	3/07/02	54%
AMEX Bull Percent	Bull Confirmed	3/15/02	52%
% Above 30	Bull Confirmed	2/13/02	74%
% Above 10	Bear Confirmed	3/25/02	68%
High Low Index	Bull Confirmed	2/27/02	84%
OTC High Low Index	Bull Confirmed	3/05/02	86%
Sector	Status	Date	Level
Aerospace Airline	Bull Confirmed	11/19/01	80%
Autos & Parts	Bull Confirmed	1/4/02	82%
Banks	Bear Correction	11/19/01	84%
Biomedics/Genetics	Bull Confirmed	3/06/02	44%
Building	Bull Confirmed	12/20/01	72%
Business Products	Bull Confirmed	2/28/02	76%
Chemicals	Bull Confirmed	1/16/02	48%
Computers	Bull Confirmed	3/05/02	44%
Drugs	Bull Confirmed	3/06/02	50%
Electronics	Bull Confirmed	3/05/02	48%
Finance	Bull Confirmed	3/15/02	66%
Food Beverages/Soap	Bear Correction	10/30/01	68%
Forest Prods/Paper	Bull Confirmed	3/19/02	70%
Gaming	Bull Confirmed	3/11/02	72%
Healthcare	Bull Confirmed	3/18/02	52%

Household Goods	Bull Confirmed	2/22/02	76%
Insurance	Bull Confirmed	2/13/02	72%
Internet	Bull Confirmed	3/05/02	36%
Latin America	Bull Alert	11/8/01	52%
Leisure	Bull Confirmed	3/05/02	68%
Machinery and Tools	Bull Confirmed	3/01/02	68%
Media	Bull Confirmed	3/05/02	60%
Metals Non Ferrous	Bull Confirmed	3/12/02	66%
Oil	Bull Confirmed	2/27/02	64%
Oil Service	Bull Confirmed	12/26/01	78%
Precious Metals	Bull Confirmed	3/26/02	74%
Protection Safety Eq	Bear Correction	2/27/02	56%
Real Estate	Bull Confirmed	12/10/01	78%
Restaurants	Bull Confirmed	1/25/02	76%
Retailing	Bull Confirmed	3/04/02	72%
Savings & Loans	Bear Correction	11/26/01	82%
Semiconductors	Bull Alert	3/04/02	60%
Software	Bull Confirmed	3/04/02	46%
Steel/Iron	Bull Confirmed	1/4/02	72%
Telephone	Bull Confirmed	3/07/02	32%
Textiles / Apparel	Bull Confirmed	1/4/02	74%
Transports / Non Air	Bull Confirmed	3/04/02	74%
Utilities / Electri	Bull Confirmed	3/05/02	60%
Utilities / Gas	Bull Confirmed	3/20/02	62%
Wall Street	Bull Confirmed	3/04/02	64%
Waste Management	Bull Confirmed	3/12/02	52%

What Does This Chart Tell Us? What Are The Six Basic Risk Levels?

1. '**Bull Confirmed**' is the strongest of conditions where we should be aggressively buying the strongest underlying common stocks in this sector. This type of market occurs when the bullish percent gives a 'buy' signal by exceeding a previous column of X's or rises above the 50% level. Rising above the 50% level simply suggests that since more stocks are on 'buy' signals than are on 'sell' signals, the probability is higher prices for this sector. Single 'buy' signals on the trend chart of common stocks can be followed.

2. '**Bull Alert**' takes place when the bullish percent rises more than 6% from beneath the 30% level to above that critical level, but not to exceed a previous top or the 50% level. At this stage many stocks are making their lows, but this reversal to the upside suggests that most lows have been made and the probability is higher prices from there. Investors can begin buying again here, but cautiously. Trading profits of 10-15% should be taken, because many stocks may retest their lows before an extended bull-market trend is established. Stocks giving 'sell' signals should be avoided. The same action happens at tops; stocks have a tendency to retest their highs before an extended bear trend is established.

3. '**Bull Correction**' suggests that the bull trend in this sector is going into a period of correction, but the trend higher is likely to resume shortly. It is characterized by a 6% reversal down from a Bull Confirmed status but taking place below the 70% level. This change in risk is telling us that the market leaders will likely drop in price due to profit taking. Traders should be prepared to buy common

stock on the next 6% reversal to the upside in the bullish percent index. The bull market in this sector is still OK; it is just taking a rest.

4. '**Bear Confirmed**' status is characterized by the bullish percent index penetrating a previous bottom or declining below the 50% level. Declining below the 50% level simply suggests that since more stocks are on 'sell' signals than on 'buy' signals the probability is lower prices. We never second-guess this risk level. Aggressive traders can establish short positions in some of the stocks in the sector.

5. '**Bear Alert**' status occurs when the bullish percent drops below 70% without penetrating a previous bottom. When this happens it suggests that the market is in a corrective phase. These corrections usually bring the bullish percent down to the 50% level or so. A 6% reversal back up in the columns of X's will put the sector back in a Bull Confirmed status.

In the Bear Alert market, you must be more defensive with your stocks and you may wish to raise any sell stop orders you have on stocks you own, so that you are sold out of them promptly if the market does weaken dramatically. Short positions can be established in some of the common stocks underlying the sector. A trader's approach should be taken at this risk level. Short positions should be liquidated on the next 6% reversal to the upside in this index.

Investors must be nimble because the market will eventually revert back to Bull Confirmed or slip into Bear Confirmed status. If the market slips into Bear Confirmed status, the short positions should be held and should prove extremely profitable. If the bullish percent reverts back to

Bull Confirmed status, the short positions should be liquidated and more emphasis placed on trading the upside with the strong stocks in the sector.

6. '**Bear Correction**' status is a pause in a bear-market type trend within the sector. Here stocks will retrace some of their decline. This phase is characterized by a 6% reversal up from a Bear Confirmed status above the 30% level. The only action taken here is simply to hedge existing short positions for the duration of the correction. Typically the bear trend will resume in the near term.

You could compare the movement of the bullish percent to the tactical strategies of a soccer game. In a soccer game there is a time to be offensive on the field and a time to play more defensively. Investing is very similar and need not be more complicated. When the sector is supporting higher prices as evidenced by the bullish percent rising in a column of X's, it is time for the investor to be more aggressive and shoot for the goal. When the bullish percent reverses into a column of O's and begins to decline it is time for the investor to stop trying to score goals and to place more emphasis on keeping the sector from scoring against him.

The bullish percent index will help investors know when to play offense and when to play defense. The sector bullish percent simply illustrates the prevailing risk in that particular group of stocks. Within the confines of a bull or bear market, sectors continually rotate. They come in and out of season like vegetables in a supermarket. The idea is to select the sectors for purchase as they come in season not out. The bullish percent index is your coach, follow his advice and you will have superior results.

For more detailed information on this kind of sector analysis and 'Point and Figure' charting, we would highly recommend you see www.dorseywright.com The best book on the subject in the author's opinion is *Point & Figure Charting: The Essential Application for Forecasting & Tracking Market Prices* by Tom Dorsey.

The beautiful thing is that it is very simple to use the exact same investment strategy to try and isolate which Exchange Traded Funds and sector funds to invest in.

What Are ETFs? And How Can We Profit From Them?

Exchange Traded Funds (ETFs) are financial instruments that are a **combination of stocks and mutual funds**. They are not closed-end funds, they are shares of ownership in stock portfolios that try to track the performance of specific indexes. ETFs allow investors to buy or sell an entire portfolio in one trade, it's as easy as buying or selling stock. Sometimes thousands of stocks can be included in each index so ETFs can provide instant diversification. They are highly liquid so they can be bought and sold any time during US market hours.

From one fund in 1993, the US Exchange Traded Fund (ETF) market grew to 30 before the launch of iShares by Barclays Global Investors in May 2000. Before then, ETFs were called WEBS (World Equity Benchmark Shares) and they were Morgan Stanley Capital International's (MSCI) single country indexes. WEBS were managed by Barclays Global Fund Advisors and were renamed iShares-MSCI Series when Barclays launched a series of new funds based upon domestic Standard & Poors, Dow Jones, and Russell indices.

ETFs are more flexible than mutual funds as they can be bought or sold using market, limit or stop orders, just like stocks. They can be bought on margin, or sold short, like many other stocks. However, unlike stocks, ETFs can be sold short more easily. When using margin, we must remember that leverage can work both ways: it can help you make money and help you lose money. So before doing any trading on margin, **please make sure that you fully understand the risks** associated with leveraged investing.

ETF management fees are typically lower than those of actively managed mutual funds because index management requires less costly research and trading. However, if you are working with a professional advisor who is guiding you move in and out of these ETFs, he or she will charge you an annual management fee in addition to the small fees charged by the ETFs.

The following market and sector ETFs are presently available:

IBB = NASDAQ Biotech Index Fund, ICF = Cohen & Steers Realty Majors Index Fund, IDU = Dow Jones U.S. Utilities Sector Index, IEV = S&P Europe 350 Index Fund, IGM = Goldman Sachs Technology Index Fund, IGN = Goldman Sachs Technology Industry Multimedia Networking Index, IGV = Goldman Sachs Technology Industry Software Index, IGW = Goldman Sachs Technology Industry Semiconductor Index, IJH = S&P MidCap 400 Index, IJJ = S&P MidCap 400/BARRA Value Index, IJK = S&P MidCap 400/BARRA Growth Idx, IJR = S&P SmallCap 600 Index, IJS = S&P SmallCap 600/BARRA Value, IJT = S&P SmallCap 600/BARRA Growth, IKC = S&P/TSE 60 Index, IOO = S&P Global 100, IVE = S&P 500/BARRA Value Index, IVV = S&P 500 Index Fund, IVW = S&P 500/BARRA Growth Index, IWB = Russell 1000 Index, IWD = Russell 1000 Value 350 Index, IWF = Russell 1000 Growth Index, IWM = Russell 2000 Index, IWN = Russell 2000 Value Index, IWO = Russell 2000 Growth Index = IWP = Russell MidCap Growth Index, IWR = Russell MidCap Index, IWS = Russell MidCap Value, IWV = Russell 3000 Index, IWW = Russell 3000 Value Index, IWZ = Russell 3000 Growth Index, IYC = Dow Jones U.S. Consumer Cyclical Sector Index, IYD = Dow Jones U.S. Chemical Index, IYE = Dow Jones U.S. Energy Sector Index, IYF = Dow Jones U.S. Financial Sector, IYG = Dow Jones U.S. Financial Services Index, IYH - Dow Jones U.S. Healthcare Sector Index, IYJ = Dow Jones U.S. Industrial Sector Index, IYK = Dow Jones U.S. Consumer Non-cyclical Sector Index, IYM = Dow Jones U.S. Basic Materials Sector Index,

IYR = Dow Jones U.S. Real Estate Index, IYV = Dow Jones U.S. Internet, IYW = Dow Jones U.S. Technology Sector, IYY = Dow Jones U.S. Total Market Index, IYZ = Dow Jones U.S. Telecommunications Sector, OEF = S&P 100 Index Fund, DIA = Diamonds Trust Series I, DGT = Street TRACKS U.S. Dow Jones Global Titans, DSG = Street TRACKS U.S. Small Cap Growth, DSV = Street TRACKS U.S. Small Cap Value, ELG = Street TRACKS U.S. Dow Jones U.S. Large Cap, ELV = Street TRACKS U.S. Dow Jones U.S. Large Cap, FEF = FORTUNE e-50 Index Fund, MDY = S&P Mid-Cap 400 Trust, Series 1, MKH = Market 2000 Holders Trust, QQQ = NASDAQ-100 Shares, SPY = S&P Depository Receipts, VTI = Vanguard Total Stock Market VIPERs. XLE = SPDR Energy, XLF = SPDR Financials, XLK = SPDR Technology, XLP = SPDR Consumer Staples

For more comprehensive information on ETFs and their individual stock holdings, please click on http://www.ishares.com

Making Money When Markets Go Down!

Even experienced, sophisticated investors can become a little downhearted when the stock market goes through volatile periods. The years 2000 and 2001 have definitely been volatile, challenging and downright unprofitable for the average investor. However, we must always remember that there are ways to make money in all types of market conditions. **It is possible to make money when stocks, sectors and indices go down in value as well as up,** and typically, they go down a lot quicker than they go up! Let's look at an example of how this can be done.

50							X			
49	X						X	O		
48	X	O					8	O		
47	X	O					X	O	X	
46	X	7	X		X		X	O	X	O
45	X	O	X	O	X	O	X	O	X	O
44	X	O	X	O	X	O	X	O	X	O
43		O	X	O	X	O	X	O	X	O
42		O		O		O		O		9
41										0
40										0
39										0
38										0
37										0
36										0
35										0
34										0
33										0
32										0
31										0
30										0
29										0
28										0

The idea of 'selling short' is simple enough. Instead of the normal strategy of making money by buying low and selling high, we want to sell high and buy back low. You are borrowing stock (in a margin investment account) and selling at one price today with the goal of buying it back at some later date at a much lower price so that you can profit from the difference.

Here we are looking at the Semiconductor (SMH) Exchange Traded Fund. As you can clearly see, just after the beginning of July

2001 (#7 on the chart) the fund started to form a very solid base of support at the $42 level. If you were of the opinion that this sector would continue to weaken and you wished to profit from that weakness, you could sell SMH short on that breakdown at around $41.25. That would have been a very profitable trade in this example as you could have closed out the transaction a very short time later and taken some substantial short-term profits.

Some investors like to own 'focused' offshore mutual funds that may specialize in a very narrow area of the market like biotech, telecom or healthcare. Instead of having to sell their mutual funds when the sector starts to decline (which may incur a sales charge), if the investor believes that it might only be a temporary move, they can 'hedge' their exposure to the 'telecom' mutual fund by selling short the 'telecom' ETF. The aim is make profits with the decline in the ETF which will offset the losses experienced by the mutual fund.

Why Invest in International Markets?

The United States is a good place to invest, but the The United States is a good place to invest, but the majority of the world's stocks are now in foreign countries and many of these foreign companies may not have matured to the same extent as companies in more developed nations. As these markets deregulate, international investors can often find foreign companies with far superior growth potential. In any country the 'serious' money is made in bull markets and if you are a global investor, there's nearly always a bull market somewhere.

Average economic growth rates in some 'emerging' countries tend to be higher than in the developed world, typically growing at several percentage points a year faster than developed countries. This trickles down to stock prices, often producing higher investment returns.

Developing countries can play technological leapfrog by jumping straight to the more advanced technologies created in the developed world, skipping the intermediate stages. A typical example is mobile phones, which are rapidly being adopted in Asia and Latin America, avoiding the need to build costly fixed line services.

The populations of emerging market countries are usually younger than in the developed world. More than half the population of Latin America is under 30 and younger populations are more energetic, productive and they consume more, which contributes strongly to continued economic growth.

> *"In both music and trading, you do best when you're relaxed, and in both you have to go with the flow."* Linda Bradford Raschke – Professional Trader.

We believe that an ordinary investor should have 10%-20% of his or her portfolio in these markets. Younger people should be at the higher end of the scale because they will typically have a more aggressive growth portfolio than older people. They can also invest for the longer term and emerging markets investing is a long-term game.

Emerging markets can involve a fair degree of volatility that investors must be able to accept. However, you must balance the risk against the reward of potentially higher returns. Over the long term the volatility tends to even out, which is another reason to stay in emerging markets for the long haul. Some emerging markets have been considerably less volatile and less risky than NASDAQ over the last few years so if you can tolerate the NASDAQ's volatility, you could probably cope with emerging markets.

You will find on the next page a listing of all the major Morgan Stanley Capital International (MSCI) Indices as of 29th March 2002. In looking at this chart remember that if you had been able to make money when the markets went down (when you 'sell short') as well as up ('long'), your overall return would have been substantially higher than if you only focused on trying to make money when markets go higher. However, even after two very challenging years for most stock markets, the ten-year average returns for 'long only' investors in some indices are very attractive:

International Indices 29th March 2002	10 Year Annual Return	10 Year Annual Return
THE WORLD INDEX	8.20	7.46
NORTH AMERICA	11.03	10.87
EAFE	5.93	4.25
EMU	11.62	7.74
EUROPE	11.05	7.87
NORDIC COUNTRIES	16.99	12.07
PACIFIC	-0.06	-1.15
FAR EAST	-1.62	-1.65
G7	7.81	7.44
WORLD INDEX FREE	8.20	7.46
EAFE	5.92	4.25
PACIFIC FREE	-0.99	-1.15
PACIFIC FREE EX JAPAN	4.30	1.76
FAR EAST FREE	-1.68	-1.65
National Indices		
AUSTRALIA	7.29	3.44
BELGIUM	8.71	5.39
CANADA	9.79	6.62
DENMARK	11.14	7.98
FINLAND	30.51	25.18
FRANCE	10.98	7.73
GERMANY	9.96	6.62
HONG KONG	5.28	5.20
IRELAND	9.84	5.76
ITALY	12.20	5.87
JAPAN	-2.08	-2.03
LUXEMBOURG	8.06	4.75
NETHERLANDS	13.65	10.19
NORWAY	7.50	4.20
PORTUGAL	9.86	4.68
SPAIN	13.90	7.20
SWEDEN	17.18	10.90
SWITZERLAND	14.24	12.95
UNITED KINGDOM	8.25	6.12
USA	11.11	11.11

Many experts feel that the outlook for 'emerging markets' in the next three to five years is good. Investors are becoming more global and are now beginning to migrate to emerging markets in search of higher returns. Developing countries will also see better economic growth as they reform and liberalize their economies. In some countries, a policy of privatizing state-owned companies not only frees up the economy but also increases the supply of potential investments.

These factors, together with strong economic growth, provide compelling reasons why investors can sometimes do better in emerging markets. Sophisticated, risk tolerant investors looking for diversification are investing more frequently in 'emerging markets.'

The following Exchange Traded Funds (ETFs) are available for you to trade should you feel that the markets in one particular country are due to move substantially higher or lower:

EWA = Australia, EWC = Canada, EWD = Sweden, EWG = Germany, EWH = Hong Kong, EWI = Italy, EWJ = Japan, EWK = Belgium, EWL = Switzerland, EWM = Malaysia (Free), EWN = Netherlands, EWO = Austria, EWP = Spain, EWQ = France, EWS = Singapore, EWT = Taiwan, EWU = United Kingdom, EWW = Mexico (Free), EWY = South Korea, EWZ = Brazil, EZU = EMU

So how do we use this information to make money?

Ten Steps To Investment Success:

1. Evaluate the market to determine the overall trend of the market. The New York Stock Exchange (NYSE) Bullish Percent Index is an indicator we consider to be extremely reliable. This answers the question - Should we be defensive or aggressive in our investing?

2. Evaluate the sectors to determine which sectors have the greatest potential for investment and select a group of fundamentally sound stocks or funds in this specific sector.

3. Preferably select stocks that have turned positive on their relative strength* within the past six months and examine their point and figure charts to isolate the highest probability chart formations. If possible, we also prefer buying company stocks where the officers of the company are buying new shares of their own stock (not exercising options).

4. Buy stocks or funds in sectors below the 50% level on their bullish percent indices (see Sector Analysis pages) and in one of the three buy modes. Also possible to sell stocks or ETFs short in sectors above the 70% level and in one of the three bearish modes.

5. Select entry and set risk management stops. Protect profits where the underlying sector has risen above the 70% level and subsequently reversed down.

6. If you buy a stock or a fund and it rises 30%, you may wish to take some profits by selling a third of your position. If it rises 50% take another third off. Hold the remainder until the relative strength* turns negative or

the stock or fund declines to the level where you took the first third off.

7. If you buy a stock or fund and it immediately declines 15%, sell it if it is under-performing the broad averages.

8. Only buy a stock or fund that is trading above its bullish support line* and only sell short when it is trading below its bearish resistance line*.

9. Remember to diversify and spread your risk.

10. With this disciplined system you know what to do when things go right and, just as importantly, you know what to do when things go wrong.

* The **relative strength** is calculated by evaluating the performance of your investment relative to a market average. Ideally you want your telecommunications stock to perform better than, or at least as well as the telecommunications sector as a whole. The relative strength will turn negative when your stock starts under-performing the overall sector. This is also when you should sell the stock.

* The **bullish support line** is a trend line that goes from the lowest O and diagonally connects each box upward at a 45-degree angle. The **bearish resistance line** will always be the reciprocal of the 45-degree angle or a 135-degree angle.

> *"The greater the number of useful things you can look at, the greater you increase your odds."* Steve Watson – Professional Trader.

This high probability strategy isolates only the highest probability trades amongst the **fundamentally strong** stocks that you want to own and funds of all kinds. In taking advantage of these 'high-probability' ideas in both bull and bear markets, you should be way ahead of the game compared to the majority of investors (and their advisors) who rarely perform as well as the overall market.

You can also use this simple strategy to guide you when investing in and getting out of government bonds and funds that specialize in government bonds.

The bottom line is that investing does not have to be complicated at all. If there are two equally great companies that you are considering investing in and after looking at their charts, we see that one has a 87.9% chance of moving higher whilst the stock on the other chart looks like it is about to fall off a cliff; which one would you invest in? Obvious, isn't it!

10

Advantages & Disadvantages Of Mutual Funds.

Mutual funds can offer instant diversification. Funds can reduce risk by spreading it or diversifying among many different investments. When buying many different stocks, if one stock performs badly the impact on the overall portfolio of hundreds, sometimes thousands, of stocks is limited. Funds can also reduce risk by investing in a number of different assets: domestic and international stocks and bonds, cash and other securities. Individual investors who desire to achieve the same level of diversification would have to own, understand and have the time to monitor more investments than is really possible.

Mutual funds allow individual investors **access to some of the world's most experienced and professional investment managers** and provide ways of targeting sectors and specific goals. Well-diversified international funds also offer a way of investing globally without worrying about currency or political risks. Fund companies hire experts who understand the complicated capital markets outside the United States, who can give a deeper insight into foreign businesses and can follow and react to news in those markets faster than most individuals. Fixed-income funds also fulfill very distinct purposes and index or sector funds can ensure that an investor matches the performance of the overall market (or sector) year after year.

> *"I feel my success comes from my love of the markets. I am not a casual trader. It is my life. I have a passion for trading."* Ed Seykota – Professional Trader.

A mutual fund is normally a very liquid investment for individuals. If cash is needed in a hurry an investor can always sell fund shares and get that day's closing price. There is no need to worry about finding a buyer or at what price the shares might sell.

Mutual fund companies often offer an array of attractive free services for shareholders: reinvestment of dividends and distributions, the ability to transfer between funds in a family, systematic investment and detailed record keeping. A mutual fund relieves you from the day-to-day monitoring that would be required in managing your own individual stock portfolio.

Disadvantages of Mutual Funds.

Mutual funds obviously have to make money themselves and they do charge a variety of fees and expenses. All mutual funds, domestic and offshore, have fees for management and operating expenses, which typically range from 1-3% per annum. Many funds also charge an upfront sales fee (known as a 'load') of 3-5%. These expenses can impact an investor's return and must be carefully examined.

Large funds can become so big that it's hard for them to find investments that provide enough liquidity. Fidelity's largest domestic US mutual fund, the Magellan fund, has assets of nearly $80 billion dollars so Magellan has to take a very large position in the stocks it holds in order to provide an adequate return, which reduces the number of potential investments it can choose from.

> *"I have noticed that everyone who has ever told me that the markets are efficient is poor."*
> Larry Hite – Professional Trader.

Another disadvantage of mutual funds is that there are now thousands to choose from and it's nearly impossible to tell if the fund is a good value at any particular point in time. Unlike stocks, where it is possible to tell if a stock is undervalued according to any of several different measures, it is much harder to determine if a mutual fund's Net Asset Value (NAV) represents a good value or not. A fund could have shown a solid rate of return for a particular period, but that could be a result of its holdings having reached peaks from which they might then decline.

A fund is only as good as its management and fund managers can change. Some funds have performed badly when a dynamic and talented manager has left so you need to monitor the situation and remember that 'past performance is no indication or guarantee of future results.'

This disclaimer is a reminder that **last year's hot fund may be this year's big loser**. An informed investor needs to be aware of the drawbacks and the advantages of mutual funds. The investor who has clear goals and who does his or her homework will inevitably succeed. Finding a winning fund takes care; read about the fund, examine the fund's holdings, understand the fund manager's style and their strategy. Ensure that the fund's style and strategy fits your goals. If you are convinced that a particular stock or sector is about to make a dramatic recovery, do your homework on which fund manager you think will do the best job for you before the sector starts to move and then wait for the right time to invest.

> *"Wait for the right trade to come along. Never trade for trading's sake. Have the patience to sit on your money until the high probability trade sets up exactly right."* James B. Rodgers Jr. – Professional Trader.

What's The Difference Between Mutual Funds & Hedge Funds?

Regular mutual fund managers are salaried employees of a firm and they invest according to strict guidelines. They are normally paid a bonus based on the total assets under management whether they make you money or not. They are normally 'long only' and fully invested at all times which means that they can only make you money when markets go higher.

However, a few of the world's most successful portfolio managers have stopped being 'employees' of mutual fund companies and have become 'owners' of their own offshore hedge funds. These hedge fund managers often have the bulk of their personal net worth tied up in their own fund and as 'owners' they have a definite interest in making money and not losing it. Many hedge funds charge '2 & 20' which means they will charge 2% per annum to cover the costs of managing the portfolio and they will keep 20% of the net annual gains in the portfolio. **This is how world-famous hedge fund managers like George Soros and Julian Robertson became billionaires.**

> *"Currently, the biggest misconception is the widespread belief that it is easy to make a living trading in the stock market."* Stuart Walton – Professional Trader.

Some mutual funds and hedge funds have similar investment strategies. However, the majority of mutual funds have a 'long only' investment objective which means they invest in something, watch it go higher (hopefully) then sell it at a profit. There is little activity in down or sideways moving markets. On the other hand, hedge funds are often more flexible and may switch between stocks, bonds, commodities, currencies, futures, options and can react quickly to changes in the market place enabling them to potentially profit from a wider range of market conditions and a broad range of financial instruments.

Some funds may use leverage. Another growing trend is the offering of a 'principal guarantee.' This is where a major bank or insurance company will guarantee that even under the worst of circumstances your initial investment will be returned to you after a certain period (normally five years).

In bull markets, the best hedge funds tend to perform as well as, if not slightly better than, the best mutual funds. In weak markets the best hedge fund managers tend to significantly out-perform the best performing mutual funds. This is because it doesn't just 'sit there,' they are just as comfortable 'shorting' the market and making money as markets fall as they are going long and making money as markets rise.

According to www.vanhedge.com a leading authority on onshore and offshore hedge funds from 1988-2000, the average 'aggressive growth' offshore hedge fund achieved a net return of 21% per annum; the average offshore equity fund achieved 16% per annum; whilst the average Morningstar equity mutual fund achieved 13.3% per annum; and the S&P 500 returned 16.7% during the same period.

Where hedge funds really seem to shine is in tough times. During the same period 1988-2000, if you look at all of the bear market periods experienced by the S&P 500 you will see that the average hedge fund was down only -0.2% where the average Morningstar equity mutual fund was down –43.8% and the S&P 500 was down –41.2%. Over the long-term, those kinds of discrepancies can make a huge difference in your portfolio.

In a nutshell, the majority of mutual funds will make money only when markets go higher, but the best hedge funds will make money when markets go higher and also when markets go lower. Just as importantly, although a mutual fund manager will often make money whether you make money or not, a hedge fund manager will only make serious money after he's made serious money for you.

The bad news is that many of the best hedge funds are closed to new investors and often have extremely high minimum investments ranging from US$50K to US$10 million, depending on the manager.

The good news is that there are more and more choices for the mutual fund investor so that he or she can also profit in up and also in down markets.

How The Wealthy Stay Wealthy With Rising Capital Guaranteed Hedge Funds

There is a new breed of hedge fund that is becoming increasingly popular amongst wealthy, sophisticated, international investors. This is a type of hedge fund where the fund management company has entered into a contract with a major bank or insurance company so that whatever happens at maturity (normally five years), the investor is guaranteed that, at a minimum, the investor will receive his net initial investment or the net asset value of the fund (whichever is greater) at maturity.

One recent capital guaranteed fund we examined for a client featured Alan Miller as the manager. Alan Miller is widely recognized as the best investment manager for equities in the United Kingdom. Over the past few years in a very tough market indeed, Miller averaged 33% per annum compared to the London Stock Exchange index (FTSE), which averaged 8.5% during the same period. So far his strategy has made money in both good and bad markets.

This hedge fund is a 'long' and 'short' equity fund. The fund focuses primarily on investing in undervalued companies from amongst the 350 companies listed on the London Stock Exchange, (English and many multinational company stocks) with good cash flow, profits growth and exceptional management. The fund will sell short companies it considers to be overvalued or ones that may be having financial difficulties. This means that it can potentially make money when stocks go up and also when stocks go down. The fund does everything possible to avoid unintended portfolio risk and his strategy has been very successful.

The United Kingdom hedge fund managed by Alan Miller was up 56.37% in 1997 (compared to the London FTSE up 17.41%); up 34.08% in 1998 (compared to the FTSE up 10.91%); up 39.86% in 1999 (compared to the FTSE up 21.25%); up 19.59% in 2000 (compared to the FTSE down −7.97%); and up 6.41% in 2001 (compared to the FTSE down -15.41%). Unlike many hedge funds of this calibre, the minimum investment for this fund was only US$50K

This track record is especially impressive since most funds have been losing money in recent years. What made this fund even more unique was there was rising guaranteed return of principal, guaranteed by HSBC Bank, one of the largest banks in the world and part of the HSBC Group with 5,000 offices in 78 countries and assets of US$691 billion. This means that regardless of the fund's performance, a minimum of 100% of your initial net investment will be repaid to you at maturity (five years). If history is anything to go by, this fund should continue to outperform the major market indices in bull markets and more importantly, also bear markets.

Mistakes To Avoid in Mutual Fund Investing

Not having a strategy is probably the most frequent mistake in any kind of investing including mutual funds. Many individuals select specific mutual funds without giving much thought to an asset allocation strategy. The investor may actually define and identify their investment objectives, but then skip the next vital step in establishing a successful mutual fund portfolio -- which is creating a detailed asset allocation strategy.

Every investor has different needs: some may require their investments are easy to sell ('liquid') because they plan on buying a car or a home soon; parents may wish to start investing for their child's education in the US; some may have possible estate planning concerns or nursing care requirements for elderly parents.

Establishing a time horizon for achieving your objectives is critical. You also need to consider your risk tolerance. Long-term investors should be less concerned about short-term market fluctuations; shorter-term goals require different investment strategies. You may wish to consider some of the following:

- **Why exactly are you investing? For your retirement? For your children? For college education? For your grandchildren?**
- **How long do you plan on investing? How long can you leave it invested?**
- **How are your assets allocated at present? Where exactly is your money invested?**
- **In which sectors of the market are you most knowledgeable?**

- **Are there any particular countries you believe have more investment potential? Why do you believe that? Where are you getting your information? Is this 'objective' information?**
- **How do you feel about investing? How do you feel about making investment decisions? Do you feel comfortable investing on your own? Would you prefer help?**
- **How can you handle market turbulence?**

Huge books have been written just on 'asset allocation' but without a well-defined, appropriate asset allocation strategy that accurately reflects individual investment objectives and preferences (time horizon, return objectives, risk tolerance, etc), the selection of mutual funds is haphazard instead of logical. The outcome of haphazard fund selection is normally inappropriate asset allocation of risk and reward, which in turn leads to ineffective diversification and results in mediocre portfolio performance. Regardless of which asset allocation method an investor prefers, the important thing is to avoid the pitfalls of haphazard fund selection, develop a detailed asset allocation strategy that accurately represents your investment objectives and preferences.

Some investors have a large percentage of their total portfolio assets concentrated in funds with very high risk/reward characteristics, even though the fund types may actually reflect chosen investment objectives. The result is excessive volatility in the price movement of these funds, which, in many instances, can cause disappointing performance because the risk may be disproportionate to overall profit potential. Having 'too much of one type of investment' can occur with any type of risk tolerance, although it's more likely to be a problem in more 'aggressive' portfolios.

> *"There are old traders and there are bold traders, but there are very few old, bold traders."* Ed Seykota – Professional Trader.

Another problem that you may encounter is the **duplication of holdings** within mutual funds. Many mutual funds have different names and insinuate a different investment objective, but you will often find that the 'Emerging US Growth,' the 'US Small Cap Growth' and, that great 'US High-Technology' fund you've been reading about all own many of the same stocks. This is a difficult problem because mutual funds do change their holdings on a regular basis. Investors have been shocked to discover that even though they might own a dozen mutual funds, many of their mutual funds invest in the exact same stocks. You may think you're diversified between funds, but if they are all investing in the same stocks – you are not diversified!

> *"It doesn't matter if my opinion is right or wrong. All that matters is whether I make money."* Brian Gelber – Professional Trader.

One mistake that's often made is **chasing performance**. Investors always looking for the 'hottest' fund rarely seem to remember that a high percentage gain is normally accompanied by high level of risk and volatility. It is understandable that investors want the best return on their money for the least amount of risk, but in a raging bull market it's normally their greed that makes the decision and not their fear.

Investors who 'chase performance' become disappointed when the fund has a bad year, (normally right after one of it's best years when they first invested), and the investor sells it then tries to find the next 'hot' fund and so the vicious cycle goes on. Patient investors (the richest ones) prefer to see their portfolios move steadily but consistently higher over the long term. **The key is to get rich S-L-O-W-L-Y!**

Many investors are experienced enough to address these problems on their own and to be able to effectively monitor their portfolios. However, for the vast majority of investors out there who have companies to run, demanding jobs, and families to raise, this is where you may want to consider hiring a qualified, international investment professional who can create a personalized financial solution so that you and your family can enjoy a better life.

Which Offshore Mutual Funds Are Best For You?

Mutual Funds have been extremely popular as an investment vehicle, but with so many to choose from which mutual funds are best for you?

Looking in the *Financial Times* or the *International Herald Tribune*, there are literally thousands of offshore funds to choose from, many of which will sound familiar: Fidelity, LM Global, Putnam, Janus, Morgan Stanley Dean Witter and many more. Some fund families may have only 5 individual funds to choose from, some may have dozens.

There are 'blue-chip' offshore mutual funds that do not have any kind of onshore equivalent fund. Of course, there are also many that are managed by the same managers that manage the domestic mutual fund. There are significant tax advantages in owning offshore funds, but it's always useful to be able to see the domestic fund manager's track record because, most of the time, the offshore funds have not been around for as long as the domestic fund.

Growth funds focus on the growth in the net asset value of the fund and typically pay no dividends or income of any kind.

Examples of some 'growth' type funds are: Aggressive Growth, Global Growth, American Growth Portfolio, Asian Technology, Developing Regional Markets Portfolio, Emerging Europe Portfolio, European Growth Portfolio, Greater China Portfolio, India Liberalization, International Health Care, International Privatization Portfolio, International Technology, US Real Estate

Investment, Information Age, Worldwide Health Sciences, Asian Special Situations, Hong Kong & China, Latin America, Pacific, Southeast Asia, US Large-Cap Stock, Global Life Sciences, Asian Dragon Portfolio, U.S. Value, Emerging Markets Debt, Asian Property, European Property, European Value Equity, Global Small Cap Equity, Global Technology, Japanese Equity, US Real Estate Securities, Emerging Information Sciences, Euromarket Growth, Korean and Thailand funds.

> *"A successful trader is rational, analytical, able to control emotions, practical, and profit oriented."* Monroe Trout – Professional Trader.

Income funds invest so that on a monthly, quarterly, semi-annual or annual basis their investors receive income in the form of a dividend. This dividend can be taken out of your account or reinvested in the fund.

Examples of some 'income' type funds are: Strategic Income, Central European Fixed Income, American Income Portfolio, European Income Opportunities, Global Bond Portfolio, Global High Yield Portfolio, US High Yield Portfolio, Senior Floating-Rate, US Dollar Bond, US Intermediate Bond, US Treasury Money and US Government Bond funds.

Sector funds would be in some of the following 'specialized' areas: Telecommunications, healthcare, biotechnology and Energy funds. **International funds** would typically invest in non-US stock markets and **Emerging** market funds would invest in stocks in 'developing' countries not unlike Costa Rica.

> *"The problem is that the markets operate more on psychology than on fundamentals."* Al Weiss – Professional Trader.

Before you invest, you do need to get the answers to many different questions. For example:

- How long do you plan on holding this investment?
- Are you comfortable with the 'name' of the fund?
- Is it a 'household' name that you trust?
- If it's a company new to you, can you easily find out more?
- Is it investing in a very narrow sector or only in one geographical area?
- What's the specific investment strategy of the fund?
- What types of financial instruments do they invest in exactly?
- Are they fully invested at all times?
- Do they use leverage at all?
- How diversified is it?
- What's the previous track record of the fund?
- How does it compare to funds with similar styles?
- How does it compared to the overall market?
- What's the previous track record of the individual fund managers? Maybe with different funds?
- Are Class 'A' or Class 'B' shares more suitable for you?
- What (if any) 'upfront' commissions apply?
- What does the fund charge in annual management fees?
- Are there any penalties if you do sell?

What Commissions and Fees Are Charged By The Offshore Mutual Fund Companies?

With most offshore mutual funds, you have a choice of investing in the Class 'A' shares of the fund or Class 'B' shares of the exact same fund. The management and investment strategy of funds' Class 'A' and 'B' shares is exactly the same. The only difference is with the commissions and the annual management fees that are charged by the mutual fund company. Please note that there can be significant differences. Make sure your advisor discusses this with you so that you understand exactly what you will be charged.

With offshore mutual funds, there are no upfront commissions charged to you on the purchase of Class 'B' share mutual funds however, upfront commissions are applicable on Class 'A' shares offshore mutual equity and bond funds.

With an investment of under US$50K in each mutual fund, the mutual fund companies will charge approximately 4.75% - 5.25% in commissions on Class 'A' shares of the fund. When you invest more than US$50K the commissions start to decline.

There is no front-end commission on Class 'B' shares; however, there can be a back-end charge when you sell the fund. This charge declines year after year until there is no charge to you if you sell after five years. **It should be noted that the Class 'B' annual management fees are normally significantly higher** than Class 'A' so that where Class 'A' shares may come with an annual management fee of 1.5% per annum, class 'B' shares may charge 2.5%. You need to be made aware of and understand all of these charges.

In the chart below, over a ten year period we show a very simple analysis between the two types of shares in a $100K offshore portfolio comprising of four different funds with the effective rate of return on class 'B' shares which is 1% lower than class 'A' shares:

	Class 'A' Net Initial Investment $95,000 after 5% commissions 12.90%	Class 'B' Net Initial Investment $100,000 with Zero commissions 11.90%	Class 'A' Portfolio Plus Additional $1,000 per mth
Year 1	$107,255.00	$111,900.00	$126,563.17
Year 2	$121,090.90	$125,216.10	$156,763.03
Year 3	$136,711.62	$140,116.82	$191,097.47
Year 4	$154,347.42	$156,790.72	$230,132.54
Year 5	$174,258.24	$175,448.81	$274,511.79
Year 6	$196,737.55	$196,327.22	$324,966.87
Year 7	$222,116.69	$219,690.16	$382,329.62
Year 8	$250,769.75	$245,833.29	$447,545.73
Year 9	$283,119.04	$275,087.45	$521,690.40
Year 10	$319,641.40	$307,822.86	$605,986.01

In the far right column, you will notice what a dramatic difference an additional $1,000 per month can make to the overall investment return. Disciplined investors will always make better money than investors without a plan.

If being able to sell at any time ('liquidity') is important to you, make sure that you are not 'locked' into the offshore mutual funds, so that you can sell on any business day. **Try and also ensure that there would also be no charge if you liquidated one fund and then**

invested that amount in another mutual fund within the same family. This is called 'no-fee switching.'

On the topic of buying and selling: If you are actively involved in investing in US or international markets, you should ensure that your offshore advisor works when the markets you're invested in are open. As an example, there may be many local public holidays where you cannot do any investing or banking at all. Remember the New York Stock Exchange doesn't close because there's a public holiday on some remote Caribbean island and if you need to place a trade and your advisor is off at the beach while your favourite stock is moving higher, you're not going to be too happy.

Most offshore mutual funds normally have 'minimum investments' which is US$5,000. For young investors this may be difficult to raise however, there are a few quality 'pension' type offshore programs available where the minimum investment might only be US$150 per month. Pension programs will invariably require the investor to agree to a long-term investment program of 10-30 years however, this will probably be very good for the investor because it forces them to become a 'disciplined' investor or, face penalties should they try to cash out early.

If you plan on investing on your own, without professional advice, you must devote some serious time to understanding what you plan to do with your money. Some investors will spend more time evaluating the purchase of a refrigerator than they will when they invest a thousand times as much money in mutual funds. This is crazy! What follows is by no means an exhaustive list of items to consider. Think of it as a 'beginner's guide' to what we would encourage you to examine when considering an investment in an offshore fund.

Basic Items To Consider When Evaluating A Fund

1. Always make sure that you are looking at a current, up-to-date 'Fact Sheet' or prospectus for the fund you're interested in. Remember that dramatic short-term moves can have a significant impact on the fund's long-term track record.

2. Are you comfortable with the fund company name? Is it a reputable firm that you know? If you don't know the name, can you easily find out more about them? Is it a company that you can trust?

3. Who is the actual person that manages the fund? How long has he or she been with the fund company? Has the specific fund always had the same manager? What's his track record? If he is new, what other funds has he managed? How was his performance with these funds?

4. What was the 'inception date' of the fund? (When was the fund started?). We would prefer to invest in a fund that has a proven track record rather than a brand new 'unproven' fund and fund manager.

5. What does the fund normally compare itself to? The S&P 500? The Russell 2000? Which index? How has the fund performed compared to this 'benchmark?'

6. What are the total assets under management? We look at this because some managers have terrific track records initially when they only have a small amount of assets to manage, but as they become more successful they have trouble putting the additional monies to work and finding the right investments. The fund can get too big to manage

effectively and then the performance starts to suffer. It can be especially difficult for funds that focus on small company stocks.

7. The 'Top Holdings' held within the fund should give you a clear idea as to whether the fund invests in the types of companies with which you feel comfortable. Beware of funds that have 'generic' type names; you need to know exactly how they plan on investing your money. Some companies will call their fund a 'value' fund, but they may use a different definition of the word 'value' than another fund company. Looking at the holdings should give you an idea as to whether the fund is living up to its name or not. Knowing the holdings should also tell you whether you already own these stocks in other funds in your portfolio.

8. A look at the 'Sector Allocation' will tell you how much the fund invests in specific sectors. Again, you should feel comfortable with how your money is distributed and where your money will be invested.

9. The 'Asset Distribution' will show you where in the world the fund invests. Some markets are much more volatile than others and this must be factored into the equation.

10. What kind of commissions and annual management fees are charged by the fund? Are these fees in line with the competition? If not, does the fund have a superior track record that would justify a higher management fee?

You can find many of these answers on the Internet; however, it may also be useful to seek professional advice to help you create a diversified portfolio of offshore mutual funds that's right for you.

What Exactly Is Dollar Cost Averaging?

Dollar-cost averaging (DCA) is a convenient, systematic way to build a significant investment portfolio: DCA helps reduces your risk and helps you build your investment **over the long-term**. It does not eliminate all the risks of investing in financial markets. There is no method of investment that can guarantee a profit if you decide to sell at the bottom of the market. But a steady, patient DCA investor reduces the effects of market risk by acquiring more shares at various prices.

Buying stocks low and selling high is simple investment advice, but it is much easier said than done! Financial markets are inherently unpredictable and it is impossible to consistently choose the best time to buy or sell. **'Dollar Cost Averaging' (DCA) is where an investor invests a fixed dollar amount in his or her favourite mutual funds every single month.** You won't invest everything at the best time, or the worst time. When the fund's price declines, the investor receives more shares for the fixed investment amount, and fewer shares when the share price is up. This strategy results in lowering the average cost. Here's another way to look at dollar cost averaging using our hypothetical investment table below.

Month	Amount Invested	Price Per Share	Number Of Shares	Total Shares	Value
January	$ 250.00	$ 10.00	25	25	$ 250.00
February	$ 250.00	$ 12.00	20.83	45.83	$ 550.00
March	$ 250.00	$ 12.00	20.83	66.67	$ 800.00
April	$ 250.00	$ 15.00	16.67	83.33	$ 1,250.00
May	$ 250.00	$ 13.00	19.23	102.56	$ 1,333.33
June	$ 250.00	$ 12.00	20.83	123.4	$ 1,480.77

July	$ 250.00	$ 9.00	27.78	151.18	$ 1,360.58
August	$ 250.00	$ 9.00	27.78	178.95	$ 1,610.58
September	$ 250.00	$ 8.00	31.25	210.2	$ 1,681.62
October	$ 250.00	$ 7.00	35.71	245.92	$ 1,721.42
November	$ 250.00	$ 8.00	31.25	277.17	$ 2,217.34
December	$ 250.00	$ 10.00	25	302.17	$ 3,021.67

By spreading $3,000 over a 12-month period in equal investments of $250, the investor was able to take advantage of different share prices each month. By December the investor had purchased 302.17 shares at an average cost of $9.93. The market value of this investment at the end of December is $3,021.67 (302.17 shares x $10 share). Instead, if the investor had invested all $3,000 in one sum in January, 300 shares would have been bought at $10 per share and in December the market value would still be $3,000.

diversified 'blue-chip' growth mutual funds whose prices have moved steadily higher over the long term. DCA encourages discipline in your investments because, once you have begun, it serves as a strong reminder to invest every single month at the appointed time. With regular investments DCA eliminates the need to decide when to invest; you do so every month, regardless of what is going on in the market. DCA also avoids the temptation to 'time' the market. Some investors cannot resist the urge to try to invest at what they think is the market low and take their profits at a market high. They usually fail because pinpointing 'tops' and 'bottoms' in the market is difficult, even for the experts.

A market decline can mean bargain prices. Unless you are selling shares, a fund's price quote in the daily paper is not relevant for anyone who is not planning to sell, so don't panic if it is down! In fact, **a downturn provides the opportunity to buy more shares at attractive prices,** shares that have the potential to grow in value when the market finally turns upward. Over the long-term, it makes little difference whether the market was up or down when you began.

As a simple example, let's look at two conservative investors who both invest US$100K for 10 years and manage to earn 10% on their money. The only difference is that Mr. 'Disciplined Investor' adds $1,000 per month to his portfolio. Can you tell me how much of a difference this would make over that period? Remember that over the course of 10 years Mr. 'Disciplined Investor' invested US$120K more than Mr. 'Lump Sum Only,' but he ended up with $477,256.17 in his investment account and Mr. 'Lump Sum Only' ended up with only $259,374.25 in his account. At the end of the day, the disciplined investor had $217,881.92 more in his account. This is the power behind a disciplined and consistent investment plan. Have you written down your investment plan?

Keep in mind that in order for dollar-cost averaging to work, you must be prepared to commit the financial resources and have the resolve to make the contributions every single month. Be prepared to weather a sustained market decline, which is a normal part of the stock market cycle. This must be expected; however, **history has shown us that while the market advance is permanent, the decline is invariably temporary.**

You Normally Get What You Pay For!

There's a reason that investors hire qualified, experienced investment advisors. If you need heart surgery, you don't expect to be able to hire the best surgeon in the world at a deep discount. So why would you expect to get proven, professional investment advice at a discount or free?

I have often discussed risk management in my newspaper columns and magazine articles because the risk in certain areas of the markets was so high. If you owned some of Internet companies that were bleeding red ink, you will have seen that when the music stopped there were definitely not enough chairs to go around. A portfolio of Internet 'dot.com' stocks and you would have been wiped out. Even if you didn't pay a dime in commissions, the savings will never make up those losses. You may as well be buying lottery tickets. You will find 'experts' who will give you discount advice, but there is a reason that it is discounted.

One of the beautiful things about investing offshore with the help of a qualified and experienced advisor is the power behind the tax deferred compounding of ordinary income, interest income, dividends and capital gains. **Due to the tax-advantaged savings, you can invest more conservatively offshore and achieve a more impressive return compared to an aggressive (higher risk) investment strategy in a fully taxable environment.**

> *"Sometimes people will ask me whether they can spend one weekend with me so I can show them how to do this stuff. Do you know what a tremendous insult this is? It's like me saying to a brain surgeon, "If you have a few extra days, I'd like you to teach me brain surgery."*
> Mark Minervini – Professional Trader.

11

There's Always Some Excuse Not To Invest.

Now that the stock market euphoria that the media helped promote has finally come to an end, they are now pretending to be concerned and are reminding us of how risky 'the market' is, and how you should not invest until we have seen clear indications that we are back in a bull market. People should, of course, be aware of the risks involved in investing, but throughout history there have always been 'disasters of the day' to worry about and various other excuses not to invest.

On all of these occasions the 'gurus' at the time were giving the same excuses as to why people should not invest in the stock market. However, let's remind ourselves again that from December 31st 1925 - December 31st 2000, a US$1 investment in small company stocks (in the Russell 2000) would have given you US$6,402.25; the same US$1 invested in the stocks of the S&P 500 would have given you US$2,586.52 as compared to $48.86 invested in US Government bonds.

In other words, there will always be a disaster of the day, but historically the returns on equity investments in the stock market have been terrific. **When is the best time**

to invest? In the words of Sir. John Templeton, *"When you have the money."*

You could listen to the reporters on CNBC and CNN television; or you could wait until every Tom, Dick and Jose knows that the bull market is back in full swing; or maybe you would prefer exploring the possibility of investing when specific, quality stocks and funds appear to have bottomed, where everybody else is too 'scared' to invest when the real money making opportunities are presenting themselves.

In the financial world we will always hear of many 'reasons' as to why the stock market isn't the place to invest right now. However, **if you are a long-term investor we would strongly suggest that the stock market is indeed the place where the money has been and will be made but, as always, you will need a proven, disciplined investment strategy with a solid risk management system that works.**

12

Writing About Being Right & Wrong

Many investment advisors will tell you that they 'knew' what was going to happen in the market. Most of them are 'exaggerating' and have no way to back up their claims. Our guidance has been published in the '*Central American Weekly*' newspaper, which reaches over 200,000 people worldwide and in *EKA Magazine*, which is one of Costa Rica's premiere business publications. This is not to say that we are geniuses of any kind; we are not. What it does show you is that if you adopted a similar, disciplined investment strategy with a good risk management system and some experience behind you that you would probably have come to the same conclusions as we did.

Imagine that on 16th December 1999 you realized that *"risk management is extremely important, especially when many markets appear to be moving from one extreme to another. In the US the NASDAQ is up 70%+ so far this year. We doubt this will continue and **we should be prepared** for what may come next."* (16th December 1999 *Central American Weekly* newspaper article entitled '*Protecting Your Profits.*') Would this guidance have helped you protect some profits or maybe minimize some potential losses?

Imagine that on the 23rd December 1999 you realized that *"...**our short-term indicators have reversed and would suggest being very cautious** in putting new money in the market right now. The first quarter of 2000 could be very interesting indeed."* Would this have helped you protect some profits?

Imagine that on January 25th 2000 you realized that *"US Treasury bonds have just given their **first buy signal off the bottom** as of Monday"* (*Central American Weekly* newspaper). Do you think this could have helped make you some serious money considering that bonds ended up outperforming virtually every other investment in the year 2000?

Imagine that on March 22nd 2001 you realized that, according to the Wall Street Journal, *"there's about US$2 trillion in cash sitting in money market funds"* waiting to be invested. *"Not all of it will be invested in equity funds but most of it will and you will probably do better investing your money before the US$2 trillion is invested rather than afterwards"* (*Central American Weekly* newspaper). Do you think you might have been pleased if you invested some money at that time and then watched as **US stocks enjoyed their biggest monthly gain in 10 years?**

Imagine that on 21st September 2001 you realized that *"our new 'sell' signal on bonds could mean there's a 'buy' signal for stocks coming soon."* You looked at your 'shopping list' of stocks to buy, you placed the orders and over the next two months you were delighted to see that big, 'blue-chip' stocks like General Electric, Lehman Brothers, Nokia and Tellabs moved dramatically higher. GE was up 28%; LEH was up 33%; NOK was up 21% and TLAB was up 35%. During this short time the Dow Jones

Industrial Average was up 19.4%; QQQ (which is a proxy for the NASDAQ 100) is up 37%; and the S&P 500 is up 17.8%. These could be considered good profits for an entire year however, this huge move ocurred in only two months.

We're not going to tell you that these indicators are right all of the time, but we can tell you that they tend to be right a lot more than they're wrong!

13

Doing Business in Costa Rica

Written by Attorney at Law Roger A. Petersen. Roger has been an attorney since 1992 and is a member of both the Costa Rican and Florida Bar. He is the author of 'The Legal Guide To Costa Rica' and is a partner in the law firm of Alliance Law Group in San Jose and you can see more information at www.alliancelaw.co.cr

'**Welcome to Technology Country!**' That is the slogan on a billboard that welcomes arriving passengers from the International Airport on their way to the capital city of San José. The sign is appropriate when you consider that Costa Rica has been able to transform its economic base from a purely agricultural economy to a diversified economy within the past ten years. Costa Rica has done this by providing international companies and investors with the right mix of incentives. These **include a stable democratic government; fiscal incentives; a highly qualified technical labor force; and one of the nicest places to physically reside in Latin America**. This mix has attracted companies such as Procter and Gamble, Abbot Laboratories, Intel, Baxter Travenol, ScotiaBank, Sykes, and many others to set up operations in Costa Rica. Therefore, it is no surprise that the World Bank describes

Costa Rica as "one of the most stable and robust democracies in Latin America, with a long-standing commitment to economic growth and social development."

Once you decide that Costa Rica is the right place to establish your business enterprise you will then have to **decide the right kind of corporate structure under which you will operate**. The Costa Rican Constitution provides equal protection for both citizens and non-citizens residing in Costa Rica. Likewise there are few restrictions on the foreign investment that may be made in Costa Rica. These guarantees allow for foreign investors from a legal standpoint to have an equal footing when transacting business in Costa Rica. Obviously cultural and social matters should also be taken into account.

The main source for business law in Costa Rica is the Commercial Code that covers contracts, sales, securities, bankruptcy and corporate formation. The Commercial Code allows three types of legal entities. The Limited Partnership (*Sociedad en Comandita*), The Limited Liability Company (*Sociedad de Responsabilidad Limitada*), and the Corporation (*Sociedad Anonima*). The most common type used in Costa Rica is the Corporation (*Sociedad Anonima*) because of its flexibility, ease of incorporation and the limitation of liability of the shareholders.

Which one will suit your particular need depends on the nature of the business and the tax implications both in Costa Rica and your country of origin. **Costa Rican corporations are also used outside of Costa Rica as investment vehicles since any foreign source income earned by the corporation is not subject to taxation in Costa Rica**. All of the legal entities described herein must be recorded in the Mercantile Section of the Costa Rican Public Registry in order to record their articles of incorporation and be issued a corporate identity card.

Another alternative for operating in Costa Rica is to either establish a subsidiary of a foreign corporation or transfer the domicile of an existing foreign corporation to Costa Rica. In the case of the subsidiary they will have to appoint a legal representative in Costa Rica with full authority to bind the corporation. To transfer the domicile of the foreign corporation you will have to translate the articles of incorporation to Spanish and have them authenticated in the Costa Rican consulate abroad. All the relevant documents must then be recorded in the Mercantile Section of the Public Registry to validly operate in Costa Rica.

Once you have decided on the corporate entity that you will use in Costa Rica then you must determine whether a business license (*Patente Municipal*) is required for the type of operation that you are undertaking. This requirement is undertaken before the Municipal government where your business is located. Generally, any business for profit -- unless a specific law exempts it -- requires a business license. Since the requirements vary from Municipality to Municipality check with your local Municipal government to get a list of the requirements. Once the business license is granted you are ready to do business.

Depending on the nature of the activities that the business will carry out, it may be required to register the business with the Costa Rican Revenue Department (*Tributación Directa*). If the entity is a corporation then the applicant fills out form D-140 and submits it along with a copy of the corporate identity card, a certificate of good standing of the corporation and a copy of the identification document of the corporate representative. This filing activates the company for tax purposes. Certain activities are exempt form Costa Rican income tax, specifically those that operate in a "Free Trade Zone" and certain tourism related activities. For those that do not have exemptions the corporate tax rate in Costa Rica ranges from 10% to 30%. The fiscal year ends in Costa Rica on September 30th and all tax returns must be filed by December 31st. Personal income tax rates in Costa Rica range from 10% to 25%.

Your next step is to hire the employees that you will need for you operations in Costa Rica. All matters governing employer-employee relations are regulated by the Costa Rican Labor Code. Costa Rica is fortunate that it abolished its military in 1948, which in turn has allowed the country to invest heavily in education and healthcare. **The result is one of the highest literacy and life expectancy rates in Latin America**. The minimum wage scale is established every six months and sets the minimum wage allowed for more than one hundred different private sector occupations. Generally, the first three months of employment are considered probationary. After that, there are specific procedures set forth in the Labor Code that must be adhered to when terminating an employee.

As an employer, you must register your company as well as your employees with the Costa Rican social security system. This system provides the employee with health care, disability and pension benefits. The employer contributes approximately 23% of the employee salary and the employee 9% to fund the social security fund. Also, depending on the activity, the employer may be required to carry worker's compensation policy on their employees. The National Insurance Institute (INS), which is the government-owned insurance company, issues the policy.

Now that you have sorted out your business structure and employees, you need to determine under **what residency status you will reside in Costa Rica**. If you will be making an investment in Costa Rica that exceeds $200,000 then you qualify for investor status. The investment requirement drops to $50,000 if the investment is made in tourism or other priority investment areas as designated by the government. Other alternatives include Temporary Residency status which can be a good starting point and gives you the option of switching to Permanent Residency status after two years. You may also qualify for Permanent Residency status and you should consult with your legal adviser to determine which status best fits your needs.

Costa Rica is committed to move towards free trade and has entered into bi-lateral free trade agreements with Mexico, Canada and Chile, among others. As a member of the World Intellectual Property Organization, Costa Rica has within the past year overhauled its intellectual property protection laws to provide better copyright and trademark protection within the country.

Whether it is manufacturing or services or simply for retirement, Costa Rica offers some attractive opportunities for those willing to venture. This combined with the diversity and beauty of the country makes it an appealing place to live.

14

Living & Retiring In Costa Rica

Written by Mr. Christopher Howard who has lived in Costa Rica for over 15 years. He is the author of 'The New Golden Door to Retirement and Living in Costa Rica.' To order his latest book, please see www.amazon.com or see www.liveincostarica.com

While there are many good reasons to reside in Costa Rica, **the most obvious reason for living here is the climate**. People are tired of freezing winters, scorching summers and the high utility bills that go with them. In Costa Rica they can enjoy one of the best year-round climates in the world (72 degrees average in the Central Valley.) We have only two seasons here, dry and rainy, both with an abundance of sunshine. We rarely need air conditioning and never need heat.

Many call Costa Rica the "Switzerland of the Americas" due to its neutral political status and spectacular mountains. This unique little country offers **a real paradise for the nature lover**, the fishing enthusiast and water sports fanatic as well as the retiree. Costa Rica fits the bill for anyone sick of the hustle and bustle, seeking a more laid-back way of life. One of our tour participants remarked, "Costa Rica reminds me of the U.S. about 40 years ago when everything was unspoiled, unhurried and un-crowded." It will also appeal to people of all ages seeking to move to a new and exotic land outside of the United States and Canada and the energetic entrepreneur, the burned-out baby boomer, those sick of long rush-hour commutes and anyone seeking an alternative way of life.

But Isn't It Expensive?

Although much has been written about the high cost of living here, what you spend depends on your lifestyle. If you must have a luxurious home, drive a late model car and buy imported goods, you will spend as much or more than you would in the USA. But if you live more like the locals and watch your spending, you will spend considerably less.

The favorable exchange rate and low rate of inflation let you stretch your dollars here. The cost of food, utilities and entertainment are all substantially lower than in the United States. Costa Rica's affordable medical care is among the best anywhere. **The quality of health care is comparable to North America, but the prices are one half or less!** Considered by many to be the healthiest country south of Canada, Costa Rica has a higher life expectancy rate than the United States.

Housing is a fraction of what you are accustomed to paying. My wife and I just purchased a new three-bedroom home in Lagunilla de Heredia, about five miles from downtown San José, for $62,000.

Besides our home, we have a car and a full-time maid. Household help makes life easier. (You can hire a full-time maid for as little as $200 per month or $1 per hour.)

My son goes to one of the best private schools in the country. We eat out a few times a week and enjoy various types of entertainment. We spend a week at the beach during Easter and go to the United States every Christmas. Our monthly expenses are about $2,500.

The country's inexpensive medical care, affordable housing, excellent transportation and communication networks, every imaginable activity to stay busy and happy, a government which goes to great lengths to make retirement and living as easy as possible, contribute to Costa Rica's appeal and make it tops on the list of retirement and expatriate havens.

A Place to Invest

Costa Rica has a myriad of business opportunities awaiting creative, hard-working individuals. **It is also relatively easy to start a small business on a shoestring**. Furthermore, tax incentives and a government that encourages investments and affords investors the same rights as citizens contribute to a propitious business climate. Many countries do not permit non-citizens to own property or place restrictions on foreign-owned real estate, but this is not the case in Costa Rica.

Anyone may buy real estate with all the legal rights of citizens. Passive investors with the right connections will have access to thousands of the world's top quality offshore, 'blue-chip' mutual funds, hedge funds, second mortgages or numerous additional alternative US$ investments.

The Adventure of Starting Over

Some people move here to start over and seek adventure in an exotic land. They are tired of dead-end jobs or the rat race and want new challenges, a chance to pursue their dreams and achieve greater personal growth. As an expatriate, you have the challenge of immersing yourself in a new culture and, if you choose, the rewards of learning a foreign language. Newcomers can make friends easily because foreigners gravitate towards one another.

A friend of ours, a 20-year resident of Costa Rica, said, "My days are so filled with exciting activities and interesting experiences that each day seems like a whole lifetime. I really feel that I have discovered the fountain of youth."

Living in Costa Rica can open the door to a new and exciting life. Who knows? **You may never want to return home.**

15

Frequently Asked Questions About Investing Offshore

Why would I want an offshore investment account?

There are five main reasons: 1) Superior asset preservation, 2) Strict confidentiality, 3) Significant tax advantages depending on nationality, 4) Access to more globally-minded investment advisors and international investment opportunities, and 5) Access to some of the world's best money managers.

Asset preservation is a big reason because, with nearly 60 million lawsuits filed in the USA last year alone, if you're an extremely successful person doing business in the USA, it's sad to say, but it's just a matter of time before you are sued. There are many times when a lawsuit is necessary, but as any American daily newspaper will clearly show, many of these suits are frivolous and too often, they are successful. Unlike the investment account you have in your own country Costa Rica, your 'offshore' investment account could offer you better protection from illegitimate creditors and predators.

Is it legal to have an offshore investment account?

Absolutely! It is perfectly legal and very simple to invest your money offshore; it's the reporting requirements that can get complicated. As an example, it is estimated that there is around US$6 trillion in US source income invested outside of the US. Once again, though you do need to seek professional legal and tax advice before setting yourself up offshore.

I am a US citizen and heard that I cannot invest offshore. Is that true?

No! It is not true, but US citizens certainly must be careful in how they do business offshore, as the reporting requirements can be very complicated.

According to the newspapers, there would appear to be many Americans who have money invested offshore. Some of them have arranged their affairs properly and some have not. The key is to get the right tax and legal advice to make sure that you do it correctly. The same offshore benefits that apply to companies like **Intel, Procter & Gamble, Abbott Labs, Bristol Myers, Texaco, 3M, UPS, DHL, Gillette, Warner Lambert, Xerox, Glaxo Smithkline, Johnson & Johnson, SC Johnson, Sherwin Williams, Sony Music, Pfizer, Kimberly Clark, Microsoft, Colgate Palmolive, LL Bean, Lucent, KPMG, Price Waterhouse, Deloitte & Touche, 3 Com, Motorola, Oracle, Perkin Elmer, Western Union, Unisys and Cisco Systems** who are all here in Costa Rica may also apply to your company.

Can a US person eliminate taxes by investing in stocks offshore?

Taxes should not be the reason that US investors invest offshore because it is very difficult for a US person to avoid taxes by investing offshore. The line between legal and illegal is defined by the US government & IRS and also depends on which 'tax expert' you speak with. However, we should remember that it's difficult getting the correct advice from the IRS themselves so getting correct tax advice from outside experts that you can rely upon is not easy.

According to a report released by the Treasury Inspector General for Tax Administration as mentioned in the Wall Street Journal on May 14th 2001, *"Internal Revenue Service employees charged with helping taxpayers at walk-in sites around the US provided incorrect or insufficient answers 73% of the time..."* These questions were probably a lot more basic than questions about how to invest offshore. **This is why you must get qualified legal and tax advice.**

What's The Difference Between US Citizens and Canadians Offshore?

US citizens are taxed on their worldwide income no matter where they live, whereas Canadians are taxed on their residency. Therefore, if a Canadian is a legal resident of a country other than Canada and spends the required amount of time outside of Canada then he is not taxed in Canada. The US citizen is taxed wherever he lives. We are investment advisors only and do not give legal and tax advice so you should get qualified advice to help you with this - **especially if you are from the US.**

Why do Americans move 'offshore?'

Most Americans who go offshore do so in order to get their assets away from the jurisdiction of potential litigants. If your assets are offshore, when a 'financial predator' has his attorney perform an 'asset search,' he will discover absolutely nothing. This is great news as these 'financial predators' usually won't waste their time on you because they cannot find your assets and they will look for another victim that hasn't taken the same precautions as you. Once again, however, it's important to ensure that you are getting the right legal and tax advice.

My attorney mentioned the 'Costa Rican Circle,' what's that all about?

In Costa Rica you have access to some excellent international financial, legal and tax professionals. Their business is helping investors in circumstances similar to yours. The 'Circle' is simply a group of professionals who can assist you in virtually every area of business that might be of interest to you.

What exactly is a 'tax haven?'

As Dr. Goldstein writes in his book '*Offshore Havens:*" *"An offshore haven is simply a country other than your own. In financial terms, a foreign jurisdiction can only attract funds from citizens of other countries if it provides financial or legal benefits that are unavailable at home. Successful havens feature those big financial or legal benefits and outdo other countries that compete to attract international funds."*

And you should invest offshore because *".. when you invest outside your own country, you are no longer tied to it's restrictive laws, but instead, enjoy the more lenient, advantageous laws of another country's laws that allow you to better accomplish one or more important financial objectives."* **Remember that the USA is probably the biggest tax haven of all. While Americans pay significant federal, state, local and sometimes city taxes, foreign investors can invest virtually tax-free in the US.**

I have different business all over the world and heard that offshore investment accounts are for people evading taxes, I don't want any problems with the IRS or Revenue Canada.

Most Americans and Canadians are rightly concerned about taxes. You should not have any problems with the IRS or Revenue Canada unless you try to evade taxes; that is illegal. You would be wise to try to legally avoid taxes, not evade them. There is a big difference in the eyes of any taxing authority. Please remember however, that most financial advisors are not qualified to give legal or tax advice.

As you know, tax and trust laws are forever changing, so you must seek professional advice in whatever you do. If you're at a loss as to who to speak with, give me a call! After speaking with you and learning more about your personal situation, I may be in a position to refer you to someone who can help you. That professional may be within the Costa Rica-Canada Chamber of Commerce (http://www.canadacostarica.org) or may be in the USA, the Far East or the UK, depending on the client. Remember, like most things in life, you get what you pay for.

Isn't investing your money with an offshore firm risky?

Just as you would at home, you do need to check out the firm that you're considering working with. Visit their offices and talk with the people that will be servicing your account. Check to see if they have insurance to ensure the safety of your assets. **You must do your homework!**

How private are my offshore financial affairs?

As you are aware, it is often a very simple matter for someone to find out exactly how much you are worth. Most people are amazed at what one can discover even on the Internet. Your personal finances are an open book. In a matter of hours, someone can find out how many brokerage and bank accounts you have, what real estate you own, and can then easily decide whether it could be worthwhile suing you. There is a much 'darker' side to this story because 'personal safety' in some Central and Latin American countries is a huge problem. I spoke with a wealthy businessman recently (not in Costa Rica) who has been kidnapped three times! **If a person can easily see how wealthy an individual is then kidnapping can become a very real and dangerous threat for you and your family**.

Different professions have varying degress of risk. One 'high risk' profession is medicine. It would appear that many medical professionals invest a portion of their liquid assets offshore to protect their assets in case of a major lawsuit. Some of these lawsuits are legitimate, but as any daily newspaper will show, many of them are not.

Your offshore financial advisor should not report anything to anybody, which is why having an offshore investment account can make your wealth invisible to others.

I am very happy with my investment advisor. What can an offshore financial advisor offer me that my existing broker cannot?

It's important to note that the best offshore investment advisors offer virtually any product that your onshore broker is presently offering. But your offshore advisor can give you access to hundreds of quality offshore mutual funds which your onshore broker cannot and at the same time your assets are better protected, more private and depending on your nationality, you will pay zero taxes!

When investing offshore you can enjoy the best of both worlds.

I've done fairly well with US stocks, why would I want to invest anywhere else?

If you have been consistently profitable, you should be congratulated. You may wish to stay with American equities, but it's a very big world out there and you may want to explore other opportunities.

In the *"The Future of Capitalism"* Lester C. Thurow states that *"Instead of representing more than 50% of world GDP as it was as late as 1960, the United States now represents slightly less than 25% of world GDP."* There are certainly many opportunities in the US; however, there is more and more to consider outside of the US. If you wish to stick with US equities, there are hundreds of offshore mutual funds that invest in US equities. If you are able to invest in these funds and pay no taxes, you will be much better off that you would be when investing only in US mutual funds where your distributions would be taxable and where you would be exposed to potentially significant estate taxes when you die.

What about mutual funds?

If you prefer mutual funds, there are thousands of top quality offshore mutual funds for you to consider. As an example, you will find a listing of some of the fund families included at the end of the book.

I am a very conservative investor, can I find an offshore financial advisor who will understand my risk parameters?

Some investors consider themselves too conservative to have money offshore until they discover that most offshore investors are exactly that – conservative! They have been successful in their businesses, want to hold onto what they've made and are typically very conservative investors.

The number one priority of any credible investment firm should be to keep their clients satisfied. To do that, they have to invest their clients' money with an investment strategy that fits the client. Good communication between you and your financial advisor is crucial. You must specify your risk tolerance and investment criteria, your financial advisor works for you and should only work within the parameters that you set.

I have a manufacturing company and I'm interested in finding out if there's anything I can do internationally that would help me?

Most advisors would need more information before suggesting how any particular international strategy that might work for you. If you are manufacturing and or importing from overseas, there could be some significant tax advantages in setting up an international corporation. One of our international clients manufactures products in Asia, conducts his business through an international corporation headquartered in Costa Rica and now enjoys virtual immunity against American-based product liability claims and significant tax benefits.

I am an estate planner and CPA who has often wondered what successful international investors do offshore that they do not do with me?

Estate planners and CPAs are rarely trained with regards to what's possible offshore, which is a shame because if everything is set up correctly, there are many benefits to having an offshore investment account. That's why it's often **called the 'ultimate estate plan.'** A good international financial advisor will be in regular contact with estate planners, accountants and attorneys all over the world, and many of them will work with other attorneys as co-counsel to ensure that your offshore financial affairs are arranged in the best possible way.

When I asked my attorney about international investing, he said that it was only for drug dealers, money launderers and other criminals.

Fear, misinformation and lack of information has led some people to conclude that investing offshore is for drug dealers and other criminals. Fidelity, Putnam and LM Global each have over one billion dollars invested in their offshore mutual funds. Do you seriously think that this is 'laundered' money?

Just take a look at some of the companies in Costa Rica that invested over US$600 million in the year 2000 alone. Are these companies involved in money laundering? Of course not.

It's always good to consult an expert who is more knowledgeable than you are in any area. The key word is 'knowledgeable.' There aren't that many legal and tax professionals that are truly knowledgeable about the offshore financial arena. However, if you are going to spend money on an attorney, at least speak with one that understands how the offshore world can work for you. They will be happy to explain the many benefits associated with establishing an offshore investment account.

An investment firm worth working with will be strict when it comes to completing due diligence on new clients. A reputable firm must be 100% satisfied that they are taking on a credible and reputable new client before any money is transferred into the account.

George Soros and John Templeton are amongst the biggest names in offshore investing. Fidelity, Putnam and

Legg Mason have over one billion dollars invested in their offshore mutual funds. They are certainly not criminals and neither are the majority of offshore investors. **They are sophisticated, knowledgeable investors who are intent on protecting their assets, and discovered it was easier and simpler to accumulate wealth out of their home country.**

> *"While George Soros had slept, he racked up a profit of $958 million. When Soros's gains from other positions he took during the ERM crisis were tallied, they totaled close to $2 billion."* "Soros" by Robert Slater.

Although I understand the attractions of offshore investing, I pay very low commissions for trading. Does Costa Rica have discount brokerage firms?

Some investors do pay very low commissions in their trading; however, the majority of offshore investors feel that the benefits of professional investment advisory services -- asset protection, financial privacy and access to top quality offshore mutual funds -- far outweigh the commissions charged.

Every day there is another story about one of the millions of lawsuits filed, especially in the USA. If you were on the wrong end of any of them, you'll know that if the decision goes against you, it can literally destroy you, financially and emotionally. You will find that most offshore brokerage commissions are competitive with any full-service brokerage firm.

I am a Doctor in Costa Rica and one of my colleagues suggested that the offshore investment world offers something that I desperately need. What is that?

Many physicians invest offshore because, unfortunately, medicine is a high-risk profession. Even in Costa Rica, litigation is becoming more of a problem. Doctors, surgeons and other medical professionals are often the target of frivolous lawsuits. By investing offshore they enjoy a far superior level of asset protection and the fact that they normally enjoy a much better return on their investment dollar helps.

One of my competitors just settled a huge class action lawsuit, should I be concerned about these kinds of lawsuits too?

If you are a senior officer or a director of a publicly-traded company, you should be aware of the growing problem of investor class action lawsuits. There are many law firms that specialize in this field and the largest one has over 150 full time lawyers working on cases throughout the US and Canada. To date, they boast of 'recovering' over US$2 Billion for their clients. Legal firms 'race' against each other to be lead counsel against public companies, their directors, and senior officers so that their firm qualifies for a larger slice of the settlement pie.

As a director or senior officer of a public company **you are vulnerable** to these class action lawsuits. Every time your company's shares drop in price, a lawyer may feel that your shareholders have suffered an injury worthy of an investor class action lawsuit. This puts you in jeopardy. Most suits filed seek damages against the company and its senior officers and directors. If your company does not pay the penalty imposed by the jury, it is up to the other individuals mentioned in the suit to pay up. If you are not covered by an insurance policy, **you are personally liable**. The lawyers who earn a percentage of each dollar recovered will seize all assets that can be seized.

Can I just bring down some cash to open an offshore investment account?

No! If you arrived in Costa Rica with a suitcase full of cash, you would quickly realize that no bank or brokerage firm would take it. There are many ways to open up investment and bank accounts. Please do not travel anywhere in the world with large amounts of cash.

How can I open up a basic offshore investment account?

Once you have completed the simple new account forms it is fairly simple to open up an offshore investment account. The company you are dealing with will need to do their due diligence, confirming that you meet their requirements. They would then call you with a new account number and instructions to wire funds or transfer an existing brokerage account into your new offshore investment account.

Can I transfer a US or Canadian brokerage account to my offshore investment account?

Yes! If you are a qualified international investor, you may be able to easily transfer the assets in your US or Canadian brokerage account directly into your new offshore investment account. It obviously depends on the advisor and the firms he represents, but you would complete the necessary paperwork, send it to the transferring broker and your account will be transferred electronically. This is a simple process and should take less than one week.

I really don't want to be bothered with the day-to-day details of my portfolio. Can I find someone to handle it all?

If you prefer to have all of your financial decisions made by someone else, we would strongly suggest that you find an offshore investment firm that has a large selection of secure, well-managed offshore mutual funds to choose from. That way you can build a core portfolio of offshore mutual funds, enjoy global diversification and let the professional and experienced offshore mutual fund managers make all the investment decisions for you.

How much does it cost for me to set up an offshore investment account?

For any type of account, individual, joint, corporate or trust, there should be no fee charged to set up the actual investment account. You simply need to fill out the new account forms, allow the investment firm some time to complete their 'due diligence' and you would be contacted with your new account number. If you need a corporation, trust or foundation then you will obviously need to pay for those professional services.

How much would I have to pay for a basic Trust or an international corporation?

The fees will vary for basic Trusts and corporate services. In Costa Rica you should expect to pay under US$1,000 to set up a corporation, which is remarkably cost effective compared to most offshore jurisdictions where you would regularly be asked to pay more than three times that amount and not get any privacy at all. More sophisticated international estate planning may cost US$5K–US$50K, depending on which professional you choose to hire.

I don't need a complicated trust or a corporation. Can I just open a basic individual or joint account?

We open individual and joint accounts for non-US citizens and non-Canadian residents every week and as long as you qualify, of course you can.

16

Which Offshore Mutual Funds Can I Choose From?

You will find below just a few examples of the thousands of solid, secure offshore mutual funds that are available to international investors:

Aberdeen US Dollar Bond, Alger US Large Cap, Mid Cap, Small Cap & Technology. **Alliance Capital Management** Asian Technology, India Liberalisation, Health Care, Intl Technology, New Alliance China, Technology, US Grth Strategies, US Real Estate Invest, American Gth, American Inc, Dev Regional Mkts, European Gth, Glbl High Yield, Global Bond Ptfl, Global Gth Trends, Intl Priv'sation, Privanza Glbl Bal, Sht Maturity Dllr, US High Yield Ptfl, US Smaller Co. **AIM Capital** Aggressive, Capital Constellation, Capital Global Growth, Capital Strategic Inc, Capital Weingarten, Davis Financial, Davis Opportunities, Real Estate & Value Fund, **Eaton Vance** Emg Mkts, Grtr China, Grtr India, High Yield, Mdln Info Age, US Growth, Health, Fidelity AW America, American Gth, Asian Spec, Dollar Bond, Emerging Mkts, Europe, Greater China, International, Intl Bond, Latin America, Pacific, Technology, Telecom, US Dollar Money, US High Income, US Large Cap. **Franklin** Aggressive Gth, Biotech Disc, California Gth, European Gth, Global Growth, High Yield, Income, Mutual Beacon,

European, Technology, **Templeton** Japan, US Equity, US Government Fd, Franklin US Smaller Co's, Janus World All Cap Grwth, Balanced, Euro Reserve, World Glbl Life Sciences, Global Tech, High Yield Bd, Strategic Value, Twenty, US S-T Bond, US Venture, **Legg Mason Global** Asian Dragon, Emerg Euro Eq Ptfl, Emng Mkts Bond, European Equity, Gl Strategic Yield, Latin America, Mexico Premium, Offs Div Strat Inc, US Appreciation, US Core Fixed Inc, US High Yield Inv, US Smaller Cos, US Value Trust, **MFS Meridian** Asian, Emg Mkts, European Eq, Glbl Asst All, Glbl Equity, Govt, Growth, Glbl Telecom, Research, Intl, Strategic Gth, Strategic Inc, Technology, US Emg Gth, US Equity, US GovBond, US Hi Yield, **Morgan Stanley** Asian, Asian Pty, Competitive, Emrg Europe, Emg Mkt Debt, Emg Mkts, EU Eq Grth, Eur Strat Bd, Eur Value, Euro Bond, Euro Hi Yld, Euro Propty, European, Europe Gth, Technology, Glbl Bond, Glbl Brands, Global Eqty, Japanese Grwth, Latin Amer, Euro Bond, US Bd, US Eq Growth, US Gth & Inc, US High Yld, US Real Est, US Sm Cap Value, US Small Cap Gth, USD Income, World Equity, **Oppenheimer Millennium** In&GtB, Inc&Gt, Int Bd, Lq Ass, St Inc, **Pioneer** America Fund, Short Term, Core European Eq, Eastern Europe Eq, Emerging Market, Emrg Europe Fd Plc, Euroland Equity, European Bond, European Eqty, Europe Short Term, French Eq, Glb Financials, Glb Envir & Ethical, Global Bond, Global Equity, Global Healthcare, Global Technology, Global Telecoms, Greater Asia, High Risk Bond, International Bond, Intl Short Term, Italian Equity, Japanese Equity, Mix 1, Mix 2, Mix 3, Mix 4, Mix 5, North American Eq, Pacific Ex Japan Eq, Pan Europ Research, Top Euro Players, US Growth Fund, US High Yield Corp, US Real Estate, Putnam Emerg' Inf Science, Europe Equity, George **Putnam**, Global Growth, Gth&Inc, High Yield, Intl Growth, Investors, New Opps, US Govt Bond, Vista, **Scudder** AsiaPacific, Emg Mkts

Bond, Emg Mkts Eq, European Bond, Glbl Balanced, Glbl Ex Japan, Global Bond, Greater Euro, Japan Equity, Korea Equity, Latin America, New Life Sciences, New Tech, Str Gl Themes, US Bond, US Equity, US Hi Yld Bd, US Reserve, US Small Cos, Skandia AF Invesco Eq, Janus Cap Gr, Skandia PIMCO Ttl Rtn Bd, **Skandia** TRowe Pr Int Eq, **Templeton** Emg Mkt, Asian Dev Eq, Asian Growth, China, Eastern Europe, Emer Mkt Bond, Emerging Mkts, EuroMarket, Euro Growth, European, Glbl Balanced, Glbl Sm Cos, Global Growth, Global Income, International, Japan, Korea, Latin America, Thailand, **Warburg Pincus** Asian, Emrg Mkts, Glbl Bond, Global Eq, Post-Venture, US Equity, Small Cos.

What's the Bottom Line?

When you invest offshore with the help of a reputable financial advisory firm, you can enjoy the advantages of investing offshore with all the security & assurances of having your assets held by a major New York Stock Exchange firm:

- Superior offshore **asset protection**.

- Complete **financial privacy**.

- **Significant tax advantages depending on nationality**.

- Access to **top quality, 'blue-chip' offshore mutual funds.**

- **Internet access** to your offshore investment account 24hrs per day, 365 days per year

- **Qualified, experienced, prompt** and **professional** service.

- **Peace of mind**. Knowing your offshore investment account has significant insurance to protect your assets making you feel **safe & secure**.

It's Easy To Get Started

Getting started in offshore investing is as easy as picking up the telephone. **Not everyone can invest offshore** however, you've read about the advantages, reviewed the risks and discovered that for most investors, the benefits far outweigh any reluctance you might have had to venture into investing offshore.

Take a moment to think about how your money can work harder and smarter for you offshore.

For those of you who wish to go it alone, we've provided you with a comprehensive road map to guide you. For those of you who don't have the time, interest or comfort level to invest individually, then properly qualified and professional advice may be the best way to begin to immediately see the benefits of investing offshore.

Whichever method you choose, you will enjoy financial privacy, your investment assets are protected, you will have access to many of the world's best money managers and for most investors you will pay zero taxes on the money you make.

Appendix 1:

Onshore/Offshore Mutual Funds & Financial Resources

http://www.aberdeen-asset.com/
http://www.aimfunds.com
http://www.acmfunds.com
http://www.algerfund.com/
http://www.davisfunds.com/
http://www.eatonvance.com
http://www.fid-intl.com
http://www.templetonoffshore.com
http://ww4.janus.com/intl/index.htm
http://www.lmglobal.com
http://www.morganstanley.com/institutional/investmentmanagement
http://www.nationsoffshore.com
http://www.oppenheimerfunds.com
http://www.pimcofunds.com
http://www.pioneerfunds.com
http://www.putnaminvestments.com/index1.html
http://www.warburg.com
http://www.morningstar.com/Cover/Funds.html
http://www.funds-sp.com

The regulatory body for Costa Rican securities firms:
http://sugeval.fi.cr

SIPC information: http://www.sipc.org
SEC information: http://www.sec.gov
NASD information: http://www.nasdr.com
NYSE information: http://www.nyse.com/
AMEX information: http://www.amex.com

Scam & Fraud Alerts:
http://www.crimes-of-persuasion.com
http://www.scambusters.com
http://www.sec.gov/investor/alerts.shtml
http://www.nasdr.com/alerts3.asp

Costa Rica- Canada Chamber of Commerce:
www.canadacostarica.org

Appendix 2:

Offshore Investor Comments

"In short, Scott teaches us that the only way of profiting from securities is to follow a disciplined, professional investment methodology, understanding the real risks and rewards of each type of investment and accommodating such to the specific objectives and risk aversion preferences of each investor." Federico Carillo-Zurcher – Chief Executive Officer, Bolsa Nacional de Valores

"Scott Oliver is one of the best qualified investment professionals. If you want to invest offshore safely, privately and profitably in nearly 1,000 'blue-chip' offshore mutual funds, Scott Oliver's new book "Making Money Offshore in Bull & Bear Markets" simplifies offshore investing. I encourage anyone who is serious about investing offshore to read "Making Money Offshore in Bull & Bear Markets"! Arnold S. Goldstein, Phd.

Prior to printing this new book, our offshore investor clients were asked the following question:

1. What do you like about investing <u>offshore</u> in some of the world's best <u>offshore</u> mutual funds?

These are a few of the responses we received:

"Scott has proved to be a reliable, honest, expert, consultant and a mentor for those who know a little about offshore investment opportunities. I feel very secure investing my capital with Scott Oliver as my advisor." JCP – Regional Director of Motorola.

"We chose Scott Oliver because of his superior market knowledge in investing offshore. Not to mention his excellent quality of service which we consider remarkable. After years of being both on & offshore we have found no one who offers a comparable level of service & attention to that of Mr. Oliver." TG

"I like the fact that the communications and transactions are private. That we can work with someone that we have confidence in and that we trust. Secondly, although I am new at this, I would expect that the returns will be as good or better than can be obtained "onshore". I respect Scott's opinion and he seems to have a strong knowledge base from

many years in this field. I am looking forward to a long relationship with his firm." DG

"Offshore investing is a great opportunity for people to maximize their after-tax returns without significantly increasing their risk. I got in business with Scott Oliver because he knows the business very well and he has credentials that can be verified." GG

"You are selectively maintaining a wide spread of investment opportunities – and reducing your country risk in Latin America." Name withheld by request.

"Scott Oliver's client approach maintains the 3 P's – Professional: Professional; Professional." WRI

"Investing offshore offers a secure hedge by placing some investment capital in a country that has a far more favorable tax climate." Name withheld by request.

"Scott delivers the trust and integrity required of an offshore advisor and has the courage to stick to his opinion of what is best for the client even though it may sometimes be easier to agree to what the client thinks is best for himself." Name withheld by request.

"Investing with Scott, provides a level of confidence, privacy, opportunities as well as sophistication to my life that nothing else has even come close to." Name withheld by request.

"I like having access to a wide variety of high quality brand name fund families to choose from, that offer the kind of offshore privacy advantages that I'm looking for." Name withheld by request.

"Investments offshore provides you with several advantages as compared to local investments. Current local investments are taxable, offshore investments are not." Name withheld by request.

"Many of the mutual funds are copies of US or European funds run by the same well known US or European companies, but based offshore, rather than some obscure company on a Pacific island. This gives a feeling of comfort/reassurance to investors." Name withheld by request.

"What I like is that I have some of the best portfolio managers working for me. It also gives me a diversification that none of the local markets could offer me, plus it's tax-free." Name withheld by request.

"Scott is ultra-sophisticated compared to any investment advisor that I have ever hired in the US or in Europe and certainly offshore. There is no one like him offshore." Name withheld by request.

"I looked for an advisor with what appeared to be: good, knowledge of a wide range of offshore investments; honest advice, not geared to churning; willingness to adapt his

advice to different investing styles; compatible background and personality; with whom I felt at ease asking questions however ignorant they might be; easy direct account access and daily pricing over the Internet, so that I could review the up to date account data at any time and the account is kept with a very reputable firm; with whom all monetary transactions are directly made." Name withheld by request.

Appendix 3:

More About The Author

The author, Scott Oliver, is 42 years old and British by birth. After his academic years, Oliver joined the elite Royal Marine Commandos. He trained as a Marksman, Intelligence Photographer and GPMG (General Purpose Machine Gun) gunner and served in many 'difficult' areas. In 1981, when he completed his term with Her Majesty's Special Forces, he joined a highly respected software-consulting firm in London, England that specialized in helping to develop real-time trading systems for many of Europe's largest investment banks. When he was asked to set up the company's new consultancy firm in New York City, he gladly accepted the challenge.

After working in New York City for some time, Scott joined Drexel Burnham Lambert where he received comprehensive securities training. He passed all the necessary securities examinations to become a Registered Representative on Wall Street (Series 7, Series 63 and Series 3). During the decade he worked on Wall Street, there was never a single client complaint ever filed against him.

During the 'New York City - Blizzard of 1996' Scott accepted a position as Offshore Financial Strategist with a firm in the Cayman Islands and four years later started his own investment advisory firm – Consultores Britanicos S.A. in Costa Rica.

Scott's professional services have been recommended in books, he has written numerous newsletters, newspaper and magazine articles and was even mentioned some years ago in Forbes Magazine attending an intensive 'Peak Performance' trading course. Over the years he has developed an extremely disciplined investment strategy for both stocks and mutual funds.

Scott helps many Canadian investors living in Costa Rica and is a Silver Sponsor of the Costa Rica-Canada Chamber of Commerce. The Chamber of Commerce is a non-profit organization that promotes commercial, cultural and interpersonal relationships between Costa Rica and Canada. More detailed information can be found at (www.canadacostarica.org) (References on Scott Oliver and his firm can also be obtained from the Chamber).

Should you require further information, upon request, you will be able to see the following documentation:

Letter of Confirmation. Written by a NASD/SIPC New York brokerage firm confirming the training, qualifications and background of the author and the safety (including SIPC insurance) of all client assets.

Media References:

'*Costa Rica Outdoors*' magazine featured the author's full-page article entitled '*Offshore Investment Provides Advantages*' in June 2000. Another article entitled '*Fishing For Tax-Free Profits*' published in January 2002 and '*Finding Your Offshore Money Honey Hole*' published in April 2002.

'***Central American Weekly***' Newspaper. The author has written over 60 different newspaper articles as part of the newspaper's '*Managing Your Wealth Offshore*' column with a circulation of over 200,000 people worldwide.

'***EKA Magazine.***' The author has written many articles on '*international*' investments for this Costa Rican business magazine.

Costa Rica's '***Friends***' magazine featured the author's four page article entitled "*Learn the Secrets to Investing Offshore Safely, Privately & Profitably*' in October 2000.

'***How To Protect Your Money Offshore.***' A book written by Dr. Arnold Goldstein in which he personally recommended the author.

Forbes Magazine Article. An article from Forbes Magazine which featured Dr. Van Tharp's '*Peak Performance Trading*' seminar, attended by professional traders from all over the world, including the author.

'***Relatively Speaking***' Newsletter. A newsletter in which the author wrote an article called '*Thinking Offshore.*'

'***Affluent Advisor***'. A newsletter column written by the author.

'***Financial Privacy Reporter***'. Another newsletter column written by the author.

'***Live Tax Free in Canada***'. A guidebook written by Adam Starchild in which he recommends the author.

'Investor's Guide for Making MegaBucks on Mergers' A book written by Richard Maturi which includes a page on *"Making Money with M&A"* (Mergers & Acquisitions) written by the author.